Is magic ~~safe?~~

Why do some people think Wiccans are Satanists?

What about sex?

How do you make friends with spirits and little people in the local woods?

Why can't I tell anyone I'm a Witch?

What are story blessings?

How do other families handle the holidays?

Why am I alive?

What will happen when I die?

Why do bad things happen?

What's all this about living mythically, anyway?

Find out how one Wiccan family answers these and other questions that intrigue pagans and their children the world over. If you've ever wondered how to introduce your children to the principles of Witchcraft, or how to tell your parents you're a Wiccan, this book is for you. If you've ever wondered how to "live mythically" or how to create your own traditions to celebrate the passages in your family's life, this book is for you. If you've ever wondered what the younger generation is coming to — and what you can do about it — this book is for you! If you're part of a Wiccan family, or want to be, you'll find a lot of ideas you can begin using right away. If someone you know is part of a Wiccan family, you'll learn a lot about his/her concerns and celebrations. For pagan parents and anyone who cares about a pagan family — *The Family Wicca Book* is required reading.

About the Author

Ashleen O'Gaea, born in the American Pacific Northwest, has lived in the legendary Arizona desert for nearly 20 years. Outspoken and public as a Witch since her first initiation, she has published letters and articles in a variety of papers, magazines, and newsletters. She has lectured on Witchcraft and won awards for pagan journalism, appeared on local television and radio, and led workshops and ritual. A veteran of the feminist movement, she has also been a grantwriter and has worked with children and families in a variety of programs. A background in education and English (including Anglo-Saxon) underlies her interests in family dynamics, religious education, history, natural science, art, music, and adventure.

To Write to the Author

If you wish to contact the author or would like more information about this book, please write to the author in care of Llewellyn Worldwide and we will forward your request. Both the author and publisher appreciate hearing from you and learning of your enjoyment of this book and how it has helped you. Llewellyn Worldwide cannot guarantee that every letter written to the author will be answered, but all will be forwarded. Please write to:

Ashleen O'Gaea
c/o Llewellyn Worldwide
P.O. Box 64383-591, St. Paul, MN 55164-0383, U.S.A.

Free Catalog from Llewellyn

For more than 90 years Llewellyn has brought its readers knowledge in the fields of metaphysics and human potential. Learn about the newest books in spiritual guidance, natural healing, astrology, occult philosophy, and more. Enjoy book reviews, new age articles, a calendar of events, plus current advertised products and services. To get your free copy of *Llewellyn's New Worlds of Mind and Spirit*, send your name and address to:

Llewellyn's New Worlds of Mind and Spirit
P.O. Box 64383-591, St. Paul, MN 55164-0383, U.S.A.

Llewellyn's Modern Witchcraft Series

THE FAMILY WICCA BOOK

The Craft for Parents & Children

Ashleen O'Gaea

1993
Llewellyn Publications
St. Paul, Minnesota, U.S.A., 55164-0383

FIRST EDITION

Cover painting: Robin Wood
Photos: Al Bond, William B. Law, Canyondancer,
Ashleen O'Gaea

Library of Congress Cataloging-in-Publication Data

O'Gaea, Ashleen.
    The family Wicca book: the craft for parents and children / by Ashleen O'Gaea.
        p. cm. — (Llewellyn's modern witchcraft series)
    Includes bibliographical references.
    ISBN 0-87542-591-7
    1. Witchcraft. 2. Family — Religious life. 3. Child rearing — religious aspects — Goddess religion. 4. Goddess religion.
    I. Title. II. Series.
    BF1572.F35035   1992
    133.4'3 — dc20
                                                    92-12569
                                                    CIP

Llewellyn Publications
A Division of Llewellyn Worldwide, Ltd.
P.O. Box 64383, St. Paul, MN 55164-0383

About Llewellyn's Modern Witchcraft Series

Witchcraft is a word derived from an older word, *Wicca* or *Wicce*. The older word means "to bend" or "wise." Thus, those who practiced Wicca were those who followed the path of the Wise. Those who practiced the craft of Wicca were able to bend reality to their desires: they could do magic.

Today, Witchcraft is different from what is was eons ago. Witchcraft is no longer robes and secret rites. During the Aquarian Age — the New Age — the mystical secrets of the past are being made public. The result is a set of spiritual and magical systems with which anyone can feel comfortable. Modern Witchcraft — Wicca — may be the path for you!

Llewellyn's Modern Witchcraft Series of books will not only present the secrets of the Craft of the Wise so that anyone can use them, but will also share successful techniques that are working for Witches throughout the word. This will include philosophies and techniques that at one time were considered foreign to "the Craft," but are now being incorporated by modern Wiccans into their beliefs and procedures.

However, the core of Wicca will stay the same — that is the nature of Witchcraft. All of the books in this series will be practical and easy to use. They will all show a love of nature and a love of the Goddess as well as respect for the Masculine Force. You will find that this series of books is deeply rooted in spirituality, peacefulness and love.

These books will focus on Wicca and Wiccans today, not what was done a hundred, a thousand, or ten thousand years ago. They will help you to expand your horizons and achieve your goals. We invite you to follow this series and look toward the future of what some have called the fastest growing religion in the world, a religion that is personal, non-judgmental and non-institutional, natural and magical — that brings forth the experience of the sacredness of ALL life. Witchcraft is called "the Old Religion" and it is found present in the oldest myths and artifacts of humanity. This series will help you see what it will develop into tomorrow.

*To Avalon's past
and Grianwydd's future*

CONTENTS

INTRODUCTION

The Family Wicca Book is about society, history, magic, psychology, politics, ritual, education, changing the world and Wiccan families. Why are they all in the same book?

Because children grow up in families, families emerge from social groups, social groups exist within society as a whole, and society as a whole both creates and is created by the culture. And cultures are historical, magical, political, and so on.

The foundations of our social institutions are patriarchal, monotheistic assumptions based on the premise that unless we are forcibly restrained, we will do horrible things to each other. All the evidence of pre-patriarchal primal cultures shows that the first humans were cooperative and gentle with each other, caring for their aged and infirm, and not living as movies like *2001* would imply.

There is evidence, too, of sophisticated religious beliefs that included an understanding of the grave as womb: we have found pollen (now fossilized) sprinkled over the dead who were carefully restored, some 60,000 years ago, to the fetal position for burial (Shanidar IV, from the cave in Iraq).

No, really, what has any of this to do with children? Just about everything! In the Saturday morning cartoons and the sitcoms and the matinees, children grow up by themselves, without adult supervision or guidance, isolated in a convenient vacuum. But Nature abhors a vacuum, and in the real world, kids grow up in families, nuclear and extended.

They grow up in other people's houses and at school, in the mall, on the bus, at the park, on the sidewalk. They grow up with Dan Rather and Peter Jennings and the morning or afternoon paper (or *The Enquirer*); they grow up overhearing our conversations about each other and the world; they grow up under billboards about AIDS and crack. They grow up in a sexist, racist, greed-tilted world, with truth-in-advertising as much a fantasy as the Wicked You-know-what of the West.

Our children grow up in a world of vivisection, strip-mining and clear-cutting, a world of spectacular technological achievement and equally spectacular economic squalor. They grow up in a world where injustice is denied or rationalized, a world that doubts the evidence of its senses and diminishes the importance of its longings.

Holding on, first to our fingers and later to our philosophies, our children are trying to keep their balance in this dizzying world. So are we. Wicca has helped us; and Wicca is the magical tool we can give to our children, just as the Goddess has given it to us.

We'll be talking about lots of things that indirectly relate to kids and families, same as we'd need to talk about gardens and vases if this were a book about bouquets. Now, the language available to us to talk about Wicca and its perspectives is limited: patriarchal monotheism has dominated Western culture for a few years now, and dominates its language as well. (Which is why the word "witch" has such a bad reputation.) In this book, you'll see some effort to restore the balance, or at least remind us that it needs to be restored.

For instance, you'll see "s/he" instead of "he" or "she." You'll also see "they" and "their" rather than "him and/or her" and "his and/or hers." You'll see "thealogy," too, and sometimes "hera" as well as "hero." These are not whimsical reverse sexisms, they are deliberate and precise usages.

"Theology" is from the Greek, meaning "the study of God." It's fine to use a word with a masculine root like "theos" if the god you're studying is masculine, but if you're studying the Goddess, then you want a word that reflects the feminine nature of your generative principle. "Thealogy."

"Hera?" Hey, girls and women can be successful and their adventures can be mythic, too. This book doesn't use "hera" instead of "hero," it just uses "hera" too. We use both words because all of us can be champions in life's adventure.

You'll notice as well that we use our Craft names throughout this book. Why? Are we hiding our identities because we're doing something bad and afraid of being found out? Because we're hiding from hideous retribution? Why do we call ourselves O'Gaea, Canyondancer and the Explorer instead of Ash, Jim and Ryan?

My civil name is Ash Fariss, my husband's is Jim Law, and the Registrar of Births knows our son as Ryan Fariss-Law. As it happens, we named Ryan in consideration of our ethnic heritage and the meanings of his names; his hyphenated surname is a political as well as a genealogical statement.

But most civil names are chosen on the basis of socioaesthetic standards. You know, always put a two-syllable first name with a three-syllable last name and don't spell anything rude with the initials, that sort of thing. Most Craft names, on the other hand, are chosen with great care and attention to their historical, religious/symbolic and personal significance.

In addition to reflecting what we or our initiators see as the best of ourselves, the use of Craft names expresses our solidarity with those who cannot come "out of the broom closet." It is outrageous that any of us must keep our Witchcraft secret from our families, friends and co-workers.

But truth is still stranger than fiction, and all of us have brothers and sisters in the Craft who would lose jobs and families — or property, or their lives — if it were known that they are Witches. They *have* to use Craft names. We use them to help people get used to hearing and accepting Craft names so that eventually we'll all be using them by choice.

The Great Mother is known by many names, and so are other Goddesses and Gods, but no one suggests that They are trying to hide anything, even though They have hidden names as well as public ones. Her names are among the tools with which we draw forth Her power, and ours; renaming ourselves in the Craft is an act of power, a power that some have always seen as threatening.

Our civil names are usually imposed upon us, reflecting and perpetuating a social system that many Wiccans do not endorse. If we introduce ourselves by our public Craft names, we are telling you that we have reclaimed the power of naming ourselves, which is also the power to redefine our lives. We are setting an example of reclamation. By doing so, we offer support to others who are in the process of renaming themselves, and also their lives.

You will read about covens in this book, too, because covens are important to children. A coven can be the multi-generational extended family kids would grow up in if we didn't have to move around to follow our jobs. Coveners can be the aunts and uncles, brothers and sisters, grammas and grampas that our kids don't get to spend time with; they are the other trusted adults from whom our children learn.

The coven is a healthy group to which our kids can belong, into which they can look forward to being initiated. Scholars, other writers and healers remind us that in the absence of wholesome social kinship groups into which they can grow, youngsters will meet that need as best they can, too often in gangs. The coven is the only place many of our kids can come to celebrate what's important to them, and to find help in working toward their goals.

Covens are also features of the landscape between the Worlds, where we hope our children will one day undertake their quests. Our coven/family — Campsight Coven — finds camping a sort of between the Worlds experience, too.

One Eostara, the Explorer and I had a long conversation about feeling like we were living a magical story those three days camping. The fact is, it got down to 20 degrees one night, but our effort was rewarded because that's how magical stories go: you brave the challenge to win through to riches you never even imagined.

Not everyone sees it that way, though; some people hate to camp! But even if camping weren't our best of idea of a good time, though, we'd give it a try now and again anyway, and I'll tell you why. Camping is as close as you can get to the rural roots of our religion, a chance to go back to the Mother for rebirth without any funeral expenses! Still, camping isn't the only way to have the sort of experience from which Wicca draws so many rites, traditions and images.

Camping does offer an experience that is consistent with our historical legacy, our present concerns with the environment, and our hopes for a biospherically integrated future; most kids seem to enjoy it, given a fair chance.

If you really can't stand to set foot on the naked planet, you'll just have to find or devise some other way of recreating the ancestral environment and experience for yourselves. Explore your family's personal or ethnic heritage and forge a link to earlier cultures with it.

Bring out or find an antique, sprinkle some straw in front of your fireplace and light the room with candles. Fill your kitchen with the magical aromas of traditional recipes. Dress ethnically. Learn the mother tongue. You'll think of ways to effectively recreate your own tradition's old days — and you can always camp later if you change your mind.

A tremendous number of Wiccans today are urban Witches. We buy our herbs and incenses at the local co-op or from catalogues. Few of us make our own tools; fewer of us have even a clue how to do that, and not all of us have the inclination. We're used to meeting indoors now, and we're not as comfortable in the extremes of weather that our Anglo-Celtic ancestors endured routinely. That's okay.

What's not okay is that community is one of Wicca's foundations, and Nature is another, and a lot of us don't get much of either. Wicca is a religion of experience, yet many of us never get a chance to share the ancestral experiences that are the basis of our ritual traditions. Camping, although unfamiliar to many and horrifying to some, can be a solution to both of these problems — which is why the big Gatherings are so popular. Camping isn't mandatory, it's not an initiatory task and not something you have to do to be a Witch. It just makes it, believe it or not, a little easier.

The Family Wicca Book is about modern Wiccan family life. Remember when it didn't even cross your mind that your teacher had an ordinary life outside the school grounds? Well, people are so interested in Wicca's Sabbats and Esbats, in our ritual and magic, that even we sometimes forget that Witches live in the ordinary world, too. This book remembers.

1

What Is a Modern Wiccan Family?

What is a modern Wiccan family? Well, we're a wife, a husband, a child, and three cats — and our dear friends Faerie Moon and her pagan husband the Norseman, and Canyondancer's brother Bilbo (who are not initiated Wiccans, but often join our Sabbat rituals), and a wider group of about twenty we love and trust.

Merry meet! I'm O'Gaea (that's Oh-GEE-ah), and I'd like you to meet my family: my husband, Canyondancer, and our son, the Explorer; and our cats, Michelangela, Cleavon and Grace. We live in Tucson, Arizona, which is a pretty good place to be a Witch.

We've been Wiccan for seven years now — or all our lives, depending on how you look at it. I was still a kid when my mom, who isn't Wiccan but comes from a pretty witchy family, told me that Christmas came from Solstice. That's what I've been celebrating ever since. Canyondancer's story is similar. When the Explorer was born 11 years ago, we decided to stop calling it "Christmas," to stop describing the world in Christian terms.

My mom's family, Welsh and Scottish, has always been visionary and psychic. My dad's side, English and Irish, taught me about herbs. Canyondancer's mom and

1

her people, Irish and Scottish, had *the sight*. None of them called themselves Witches — they were everything from Presbyterian to free thinkers, Episcopal to agnostic — but they seemed witchy enough to us!

Canyondancer and I were married almost 20 years ago in a Unitarian church, and in Tucson we were active in the Unitarian-Universalist church for about 10 years before we needed something more. When we left the church, looking for something more participatory and compelling, more immediate and yet more mythical, Faerie Moon gave me a copy of *Drawing Down the Moon*.

I read it and then *The Spiral Dance* in quick succession and we never looked back. (Now, when I remember old times, it feels as though we were Wiccan then, too!) Canyondancer and I initiated each other to first degree a couple of years later, one Samhain midnight; I took my third degree from two eclectic priestesses here just before 1990's Summer Solstice. Canyondancer and I work with each other, of course, and with the Explorer and Faerie Moon — together we made Campsight a coven at Bride of 1991.

Mind, we'd been keeping Sabbats and Moons for some time. Canyondancer and I called ourselves solitaries who happened to be married and work together, and the Explorer worked with us now and again and participated in all our Sabbats and Esbats. Faerie Moon and the Norseman were another solitary Witch and her pagan husband who joined us for many Suns and Moons. Asked if we were a coven, we said for many years that we weren't.

It wasn't only the number of years we've been Witches together that moved us to formalize Campsight, though. It was also the fact that all of us are able to be straightforward about our faith, and we feel that gives us an obligation to stand up, even stand *out*, for our brothers and sisters in the Craft who can't do the same.

Faerie Moon, the 'dancer and I have talked to people about Wicca for years, answering questions and correcting misunderstandings. We've written a number of flyers to hand out when we start conversations, on the bus or with our clients and patients, that we don't have time to finish. We've been doing this work for years, along with the odd radio shows, television appearances, lectures, and workshops.

Our decision to formalize Campsight as a coven, then, was in some way political. Spiritually, we are dedicated to the God/dess; to Witchcraft's model of the world as a friendly, family- and growth-oriented place. We've earned the right to call ourselves a coven by our religious study and dedication, yes; and we have also entitled ourselves to what "socio-political" security and authority a coven offers. Officially, Campsight's a young coven, just settling into its routine — but the Gods have known us for years!

We are raising the Explorer to the Craft, and he is a member of our coven as naturally as he is a member of our family. At his first dedication, near his seventh birthday, he was able to commit to the Goddess' service in terms of respecting life and helping to take care of the environment. Now he can cast a Circle with us and anticipates another pre-initiatory dedication when he enters his teens.

The older he gets, and the more concerned with the affairs of the world-that-is-wider-than-our-neighborhood, the more he appreciates Wicca. There are still some complaints about turning off the television or putting down what he's reading when it's time for Circle, but once a ritual begins, his attention is better focused each time.

Could he be your child? Wicca's tenets make sense to him and he finds encouragement in Witchcraft's morality. These days it can be tough to make sense of the world, but Wicca's teachings are a helpful framework for understanding. Witchcraft's wide perspective, global and historical, is a context for patterns of events. Wicca's confidence in the loving nature of life and its emphasis on family guarantees that all of us can have a hug when we need one.

Other Witches we know make families of good friends as well as of blood relations, too. Some of our friends have babies, some are single parents, some have grown children and some have none; some are straight, some are gay. So what's a family? A family is any group of people who know each other well and love each other anyway! Seriously, family are those people who nurture us and affirm us, who delight in and contribute to our growth, and grow right along with us.

The family is humanity's natural social unit, and arguably the model for covens, which are representations of the cosmos. Starhawk says that in Wicca's context we can call it "love" that holds atoms together in the forms we inhabit and take for granted. Similarly, life, the universe and everything is one big family, and all of us are favorite children.

In a more prosaic sense, are we a traditional family? Not statistically! We have 1.0 children, not 2.8. We have only one car and only one income. Canyondancer tends the home fires while I work in a law office. So no, we're not socioculturally traditional — are you?

When Canyondancer and I announced our engagement, another old and dear friend, a "sister with different parents" who is now a Presbyterian elder, made us a plaque that said:

> *True love is not looking at each other,*
> *it's gazing outward in the same direction.*

This made sense to us, and still does, and it's become a part of our understanding of FAMILY.

Canyondancer and I made certain choices — that one of us would stay home with our son, for instance, even though it reduces our income — in favor of the family life we wanted. We're aware that many things would be different if we didn't have a kid, and that many things could be different if we were raising him differently. We've made all of our choices with our eyes open, willing to accept the consequences even if we couldn't anticipate all of them.

And now, "consequences," with its negative connotations, doesn't seem like the right word to use. All we've given up is a few *things,* and we don't miss any of them. What we have instead is more precious than the richest collection of possessions: we have unconditional love and peace, and in that, the only real security there is.

Our family is united by many values and attitudes, all of them directly or indirectly Wiccan. As the Explorer grows up, our relationships will change; if Faerie Moon and the Norseman move to the mountains, that'll change things, too. Change is what we worship, for change makes growth possible, and growth is what life — and families — are all about.

Your family is united by shared values and attitudes, as well, and your family is growing and changing, as all families do. All of us can find power in change, and the power to shape those changes to our will. That's the very heart of family life — and of Witchcraft. *As you will, so mote it be:* families, yours and mine, are what we make of them, you and me.

Our life as a family of Witches is full and satisfying. Wicca permeates our lives, enriches our lives, guides our lives. In this book we'll share some of our traditions, rituals, and songs; some of the problems we've encountered and our best solutions to them; and some of our thoughts about life, the universe, and everything.

2

BETWEEN THE SABBATS

No matter how many charming holiday traditions and rituals your family has, the fact remains that life is not all holidays. There are far more "everydays" on the Wheel than "holidays," and the secular Judeo-Christian culture influences those everydays. For a Wiccan family, especially one whose relatives and friends don't know about Witchcraft, it is a challenge to keep Wiccan values.

Besides "family" being defined differently now than it was even five years ago, many other things have changed. These days, most of us work. The two-income family is the norm now, and good day-care is really hard to find and pay for. We watch more television and read less and tell fewer stories than we did 20 years ago. We talk more on the phone and write fewer letters. We're more pressured to accept material standards, and we're separated by more miles than we used to be. Our children face more dangers and challenges than many of us did when we were growing up.

Yet we practice a religion rooted in a rural, communal life that most of us never experience. How can we find and live by Wiccan values under these circumstances?

Defining our Wiccan values takes some work. We have just the one Law, that what we give into the World is given back to us "three-fold." We have no books of dogma, no commandments save the Rede:

An ye harm none, do as ye will.

The "none" we may harm includes the whole of life, not just the two-foots and four-foots we call friends. What we will is not necessarily the same as what we want, so our individual interpretation of the Rede can't be as simple as it looks! Our Rede and our Law make us responsible for a morality as complex and sophisticated as any on Earth.

We have other liturgical material from which we might draw our moral code and ethics as well. The Charge of the Goddess in any of its versions *(please see Appendix A for a complete text and some interpretation)* is rich with instruction and direction. From it we know when to meet and what to do when we gather under the Moon, and from it we can learn a great deal about why, too.

From the Charge we can learn what the Goddess expects of us and how to live our lives in harmony with Hers. From chants and invocations we can infer even more, for Wicca is, as Starhawk has said, a "poemagogic" religion, and our liturgical material is metaphorical even when it can be taken literally.

Aphorisms like *as above, so below* guide us, too. Obviously the Earth's orbit around the Sun puts us in the universal swing of things. It's plain that the same laws of physics apply here "below" as there "above." But "above" and "below" aren't just two more compass points. They stand for all the expressions of duality the universe manifests, so *as above, so below* reminds us of the ultimate interconnection: wholeness!

Perception of the God/dess' wholeness is a choice. As Wiccans, we have accepted that there is more to us than our material components, which means we accept that there's more to everything else than what we can see, as well. This understanding keeps us aware and appreciative of the God/dess' work, and resistant to all the "only ways" we're urged to follow.

WICCA IN THE WORLD

Doing our parental "thing," or talking to friends who ask advice, or even talking politics, we quote and interpret Wiccan "scripture" often. We include in our definition of Wiccan "scripture" everything we know about the planet: geology, physics, biology, natural history, and other sciences; all the psychology and history we know; and all the various perspectives on such subjects that are familiar to us.

The more we understand about life, the less likely we are to do any harm when we act socially, politically and magically, so we encourage each other to know as much as we can. We have always included our son when we talk about "right and wrong." We have always explained our decisions to him, told him what factors we take into account and why some considerations are more important to us than others.

When I say "always," I mean always, too: literally since the day he was born (at home, with the help of three wonderful midwives), we've talked to him about life. Of course he couldn't understand everything we said to him at first — he still doesn't understand everything — but he does understand that he can rely on us to communicate. Because we do, he knows it's safe for him to share thoughts and feelings, to be honest and willing to reconsider, and to take responsibility for his own decisions.

The Explorer is an intelligent, sensitive young man with a delightful sense of humor and good manners. We are impressed with his abilities to analyze and to empathize — he knows how to walk a mile in your shoes.

We like to think that our own example, guided by the Wiccan principles we've derived from the Rede, the Law, the Charge, and all our other liturgical material, has something to do with the Explorer's being such a fine young man.

We know that being part of a coven has been good for him, and that our extended "Beltane family," the 20 or so people with whom we camp, is a supportive community that can meet many of his present and future needs. Also, the city-wide Wiccan community here is wonderfully varied and a tremendous resource for children and adults alike.

Not every Wiccan child can enjoy these advantages, but today's hard work will make it easier for their children. We are quite sure that any child brought up in the light of a Wiccan Sun and Moon will be a fine person.

It's not all love among the flowers, of course; Winter is real, and so are bad days and problems. Fortunately, the Goddess' unconditional love is real, too, and a resource upon which we can draw, whether it's manifest in the Sabbats or in the patience needed to raise children.

There are opportunities to teach and reinforce Witchcraft's world view and values. Being disinclined, for instance, to spend $20 for an evening in a loud, sticky theater to watch a violent and cynical movie, we watch a lot of Public Broadcasting (PBS). We find that the shows we see on this network affirm Wiccan perspectives more often than not. (We don't get cable, so all I'm going to say about it is that I think you might get some of the same shows.)

Nature and *Nova* and other animal and science shows, including recent offerings like *The Planet Earth* and *The Race to Save the Planet* make it clear, often pointedly, that humanity's place is among other life forms. These shows emphasize life's interconnectedness, and noticing the connections is a chance to point out that this is exactly what Wicca teaches us.

Even the bits about hard science — programs about the basics of quantum physics, the development of the human body within the womb, or unified field theory, for instance — are lessons in Wicca. The scientific method has taught us nothing which cannot be expressed in the Craft's traditional terms. Evolution on every scale is perfectly Wiccan, and almost everything we've ever heard on "the educational channel" can be rephrased in our religious metaphors.

Dance in America, The American Experience, Travels, Great Performances, and various special and more specific series like *In Search of the Trojan War, Cosmos, Connections,* and the later *Testament* — all these shows and more (check your local listings) offer, at least, interesting perspectives and opportunities to talk about Witchcraft's ancient and modern culture. Sometimes there's even an accurate glimpse into our history!

Occasionally you find references to Pagan cultures where you least expect them. In 1990 we watched a show about British architecture hosted by HRH Charles. Twice in the hour he referred to the value of pagan contributions to style! And when a series like Joseph Campbell's comes along, discussion groups all over the country meet to watch the tapes.

But even the most mundane shows are opportunities to discuss Wiccan attitudes and standards — about sex, death, relationships, social obligations, matters ecological, and so on. So far on a PBS series called *Trying Times* we've seen two half-hour comedies that were almost blatantly pagan. One featured an apparently Voudoun priestess administering social justice, and in the other, a comically desperate self-image was restored through the magic of a matriarchal heirloom ring.

The daily papers are another source of opportunity to clarify Wiccan beliefs and principles. When the Explorer was just starting to enjoy reading the comics, we found that many of the punchlines depended on a patriarchal, monotheistic perspective. References to the devil or guardian angels, for instance, still need some explaining.

A word about such explanations. It's best, in our experience, to give children information about other religions rather than just opinions. When they're given information without interpretation, our kids learn that they can rely on us to give them the facts and infer that we trust them to draw their own conclusions.

Many of our explanations are historical — Moses brought his stone tablets down the mountain at about the same time as the builders of Stonehenge were bringing their stones across the plains, for instance. Letting children know that there is a historical context for legendary events helps them realize several important truths, including the fact that history isn't one-dimensional, even if some accounts of it are.

The Explorer has asked us many questions regarding Christianity, Judaism, and Islam that we cannot answer satisfactorily. When that is the case, we admit it, and go on to present Wicca's relevant thealogy or philosophy. "I can't explain why they believe this or think that," I'll say. "But I can tell you how *we* look at it, though."

In this way, kids learn elemental Craft principles without needing to devalue other faiths. When we can't answer the Explorer's questions, we ask people who can. As a result, the Explorer has discovered what he considers to be a number of inadequacies in monotheistic dogma which he hears from his friends and from ours. He has also discovered that the dominant Western religions owe much to Witchcraft.

Taking this sort of sociological approach in our answers to anyone's questions, including our own, makes it clear that any philosophy that respects the Earth will develop a code of social and religious conduct that preserves it. Any system that calls our physical world insignificant or identifies it as enemy territory is likely to generate less considerate customs.

Why this matters is obvious, at least to Witches. It is better to light a candle (or honor the Moon) than to curse the darkness. But if you are so careless, foolhardy, or arrogant as to pull the wick out of your candle, what are you going to do for heat and light when the sun goes down?

A philosophy that advocates yanking the wick anyway has followers who are blinded, cold, and afraid of the dark. Perhaps one reason we're called <u>Wic</u>cans is that we have sense enough to leave the wicks *in* our candles; to accept life in its entirety rather than denying those observations and experiences that challenge us or threaten the greedy and powerful.

We talk this way to our son, and to everybody else who will listen, for this attitude is a tool that will serve any of us well, whatever quests we undertake.

Volatile issues — abortion, the death penalty, smoking, military expenditure and policy, education, whether or not to eat meat, homelessness, racism, and sexism — need to be discussed and evaluated in Wiccan terms. Even though Wiccans of various denominations hold different opinions on these subjects, your opinions and mine come from our understanding of Wiccan principles. *It is those principles and our interpretation of them that we need to share with our families.*

We make a conscious effort to share the variety of Wiccan opinions with the Explorer and with others whose questions about Witchcraft we work to answer. Within each community Witches make widely different decisions about important issues. The wonderful thing about our disagreements is that we are not threatened by them!

None of the service reservists we know argue with Circling for peace; indeed, they join us when they can. None of the vegetarians we know want to police our grocery shopping, nor do they suspect meat-eaters of sneaking flesh into "cauldron-luck" dishes. None of the pagans following other paths — Native North American, Caribbean or Nordic, for instance — hesitate to join public Circles led by Wiccans, and we don't hesitate to let them guide our energies toward common goals.

Witchcraft's emphasis on the interrelationships of Life makes it unnecessary for us to fear or mistrust each other. There are no inconsistencies in our thealogy to put us on the defensive. The God/dess' love for us is unconditional, so ours for each other and for Life can be, too.

STUCK IN THE BROOM CLOSET

If your family cannot celebrate the wheel openly, if you cannot say "Goddess" as well as "God," if your lives as Witches are bounded by community or family intolerance, then the single most important tradition your family can establish is that of open COMMUNICATION.

Your children may be too young to understand everything you say, but none of us is ever too young to be nourished by the freedom that characterizes a communicating family.

How can we explain to our children that they shouldn't talk about Wicca, about our beautiful rituals, without giving them the impression that there's something wrong about it? We think the best approach is the same one we use to teach that their bodies are their own, not for others to touch or look at.

All religions consider their rites sacred, most prohibit photographs of rituals (with the general exception of weddings), and most take some precautions against mockery and disruption. Even though most Americans know something about the religious practices of the mainstream religions, in every religion there are aspects known only to its confirmed followers.

So it is with Wicca. In the old days, yes, secrecy was a matter of life and death. In some places today, it still is; in some places today, jobs depend on secrecy. And some of us are just not publically inclined, and would not talk about our faith even if it were "mainstream."

The confusion of Witchcraft with Satanism can make Wicca's secrets seem ugly, though, so it's important that as we teach our children to keep our sacred secrets, we also teach them ways in which they can talk about religion. It doesn't come up often among children, but it does come up sometimes. "Do you believe in God?" the Explorer has been asked.

For years, he's been answering that one this way: "Yes, I believe in the God, and in the Goddess, too." Calling them Mother Nature and Father Time satisfied his friends' curiosity without causing any serious misunderstandings.

As the Explorer and his friends get older, I hear them talking about religious issues more specifically. Not long ago, a neighbor child asked the Explorer if he was "afraid of death." As I recall, the Explorer said matter-of-factly that he was not, and the conversation didn't go any further.

If it had, though, the Explorer would have been able to talk about his beliefs in terms of experience, without having to argue thealogy. When his great-grandmothers died, we encouraged the Explorer to ask questions, and we paid special attention to his speculations. We talked about what happens to flesh and bone and ether and mind, and we talked about it until he was satisfied with his understanding. And it helped me, too.

But what about the *secrets?* What about those things we can't tell other people? If there's nothing wrong with them, why can't we tell?

Well, let's put that in perspective, shall we? First, there are lots of things that not everybody knows or can do. Kids, for instance, can't drive, vote, drink beer, operate heavy machinery, hold a job, negotiate contracts, win lotteries. In college, many classes are closed to students who haven't taken preliminary courses, and nobody suspects the upper-level classes of being bastions of crime or evil.

In more specifically religious terms, lots of churches exclude non-members from their mysteries because non-members are not grounded in the faith; the mysteries would have no meaning. Wiccans do not share rituals or Books of Shadows with non-initiates for the same reason. Non-initiates — even those studying for initiation — have not been properly prepared to understand the rites.

Wicca's mysteries are the special rewards of study and discipline. Keeping our secrets is no more "sinister" than not giving birthday presents at a party to the children whose birthday it isn't! (Most children and adults can relate to a birthday party example, so feel free to use this analogy if it will work for you.)

OH, BY THE WAY, MOM AND DAD . . .

While the grandparents in our family accept that we are Wiccan, there are elements of Witchcraft they don't understand; there are aspects of their lives that we don't understand, too! When the Explorer notices differences in our lifestyles, he asks us about them. This gives us yet another opportunity to point out what wonderful diversity there is in the world.

No matter how well we are able to understand how someone else's mind works, none of us is responsible for the way another person thinks or acts. There's no need for any of us to be defensive about our differences. This concept, though, is not universal, and not everyone accepts it as true.

We think it's an obvious derivation from Wiccan belief, so if the Explorer does something inappropriate, we can correct his behavior calmly, without embarrassment, because we know that he is responsible for his behavior. We know this is true even when Gramma and Grampa are horrified, or think we're too lenient.

Behold, I am the Mother of all things, and My love is poured forth across the Lands, the Goddess tells us in Her Charge. One of the things this passage means is that Her love is expressed in everything, even in things different from what we are and what we easily understand.

You shall be free from slavery, She tells us, and that includes the cultural slavery of gender and status roles. *Naked in your rites* means without emotional masks, too. *Love unto all beings* is Her law, including those beings different from ourselves. *Nor do I require aught of sacrifice,* She promises — certainly not the sacrifice of our selves, though our social gods — and sometimes our families — do demand it!

Although it was from my parents that I first learned about the pagan origins of Christian holidays, there is still much about our being Wiccan that befuddles them. They understand that Witchcraft is very old, and that we are not Satanists, but they still wonder what we celebrate. Many folks whose grown children are Wiccan wonder the same things; your parents might be interested, too.

For people whose careers depend on an almost bureaucratic conformity — at school, at work, at the club, at home, in the ladies' auxiliary — our pagan differences are distressing. Many Wiccans have to conceal their faith from their employers and from family members, and when some of us are still persecuted violently, it's not hard to understand the concern.

Most of us grew up under The Rules, recently articulated very powerfully in a PBS series called *Making Sense of the Sixties:* obey authority, conceal your feelings, fit in with the group, and don't even *think* about sex. Daring to profess Witchcraft in a culture that has not significantly changed these rules is scary.

The only culturally acceptable way of responding to that fright is to obey authority by concealing our feelings and to fit into the group. Some of our families get angry with us if we are unwilling to atone for our "sin" of violating those rules. Some of our families are just worried that we — and they — will feel the wrath of — well, feel The Wrath.

They express it according to their own understanding: if you wouldn't be that way, these things wouldn't happen. No matter how kindly or gently this is whispered or gestured, it presumes guilt and that the problem is within us, not within the system. This kind of guilt is a foundation for many lives; John Bradshaw and others call it "toxic shame."

Even though guilt is not a part of the Wiccan construction of the world, it sneaks into our lives on little secular feet. Our government says that individuals are responsible for a dysfunctional society, just as children are made to feel responsible for their dysfunctional parents. As it has been since the first patriarchal invasions, refusing the yoke of guilt — deciding not to follow The Rules — not only can be dangerous, it makes *us* dangerous.

When we speak to our families about religion, we must remember that we are speaking to frightened people. We must reassure them in terms they can understand, in terms of the rules they've internalized. We can point out to them, for instance, that a lot of what we do looks a lot like what they do. (More accurately, a lot of what they do looks like what we do.)

One year my parents asked me whether we celebrated New Year's. "It's on the calendar," my dad reminded me, implying that if it's on the calendar, we have to celebrate it. I told him that yes, we're up at midnight on New Year's

Eve to count down with the television, and blow horns, and take a picture.

I did not remind him that Solstices and Equinoxes and Full Moons are on most calendars, too, and that by his reasoning, the whole country should be celebrating them as well. He wasn't asking for information, he was asking to have his fear of and for my differentness allayed.

There is so much secrecy, so many rumors and lies, that it's a wonder any of us know what we're doing. Christian holidays are so much a part of our culture that they are half-secularized, which makes it hard to tell what is religious and what is not. Some people have trouble understanding that there is more than one sort of holiday at all!

When I tell my parents that our religious new year was at Samhain, they think we are rejecting any secular celebration of the beginning of a new calendar year. Canyondancer's family thought for some time that because we don't celebrate Christmas, we must not celebrate any Winter holiday.

As for Halloween, many nominal Christians are so terrified of mortality that the idea of honoring death as part of the life cycle is literally beyond their comprehension. Even though it is a perverted understanding, so many people understand death as an end or a punishment that facing it calmly seems, to them, insane.

Beltane's Maypole is not such a threat. Many of our parents, and many of us, can remember dancing it in grade school, and 'dancer and I both remember Maypole dances on our college campuses (mine liberal, his conservative). Even though the Maypole is straightforwardly phallic, many people's appreciation of its spiral mating dance is based on a carefully constructed and defended "innocence" of its significance.

At the same time, the Maypole is a blatant reminder of a real and significant difference between monotheisms and paganisms. Naming our flesh evil (or inferior or illusory or otherwise invalid) creates in us a schizophrenia that begs to be healed — and Witchcraft heals.

I know a man in his seventies who said to me after his mother passed, "Now there's nobody between me and death." It may be the same death which separates us from our parents that reunites us with them, for our Wiccan attitude toward death — sadness without guilt or fear — allows us to comfort our elders as they face their mortality.

And as our generation of "boomer Witches" gets older, and we and our parents begin to cross the astral Western Sea on our way to the Summerland, we may be able to offer our parents a psychological healing and rebirth in addition to the reincarnation the Gods will offer. Wicca may not be so hard for them to accept if they find its thealogy comforting in a moment of need: there are, as World War II vets are fond of saying, no atheists in foxholes (and monotheism isn't the only non-atheism).

There are less desperate ways of introducing parents and other family members to Witchcraft, of course. Scott Cunningham's *The Truth About Witchcraft Today* is an easy-to-read, non-threatening book that many Witches have left with their families as an introduction.

Casual conversations offer some opportunities, too. "Isn't it interesting that Christmas celebrates the rebirth of the s-o-n, while Yule celebrates the annual rebirth of the s-u-n?" "Did you know that eggs are ancient symbols of fertility, and people have been coloring them to celebrate the Spring Equinox for thousands of years?" "I wonder how many people know that there weren't any real Witches executed in Salem?"

Almost everybody I've talked to has heard of "those caves in France," even if not everyone is comfortable trying to pronounce their names. (*Les Trois Frères, Lascaux:* lays-TWA-frair, laz-COE.) No one I've talked to has been inclined to call those antlered priests or the statues of "Venus of Willendorf" Satanic, either, although one woman I met at a bus stop wasn't sure she agreed that there were no Christians 40,000 years ago.

The more we know about our 60,000-year history, the better we're able to recognize and take opportunities to tell people the truth about Witchcraft. Some parents are still upset that their Wiccan children no longer practice their religion. They may be able to accept the fact that their religion, whatever it is, developed out of ancient Witchcraft, and that Wicca is an expression of their own faith's heritage.

Some parents will not accept Wicca and insist that we are doomed to a damned eternity. It may well be that the best we can do with them is *accept that this is what they choose to believe, and honor their right to believe it.* What we must not do with such parents is take responsibility for their attitudes.

As Wiccans, we know how true it is that we can choose and change our attitudes. We also know that it is wrong to manipulate other people's attitudes when those people haven't asked us to work with them. If you have trouble resisting your parents' manipulations (by prayer or harassment or threat), then you can work for yourself, casting spells of protection and developing greater strength. You do not need to let them draw you into the battles they have chosen to fight. Responses like these are appropriate when your family confronts you accusingly:

"I understand that this is what you believe."
"I am sorry that this troubles you so deeply."
"I see that you are very upset about this."
"I will try to answer some of your questions when we can talk calmly."

Remember that they are scared. They interpret Wicca as a threat to their beliefs, and they may interpret your practice of the Craft as a threat to their parental power. In fact, they may perceive a Wiccan lifestyle as a devaluation of their whole lives, of everything they worked for, everything they tried to give us. With parents who absolutely won't accept Wicca, it may be best to offer affirmations of those things we appreciate about their lives.

My mother will not articulate her religious beliefs because if she commits to one point of view, she might be proved wrong in the End. She's a world-class calligrapher, the source and nurture of my artistic bent. My father has been heard to say that he guesses he's Christian because most Americans are; he taught me the respect for life and environment that supports Wicca in my life.

When my father says that "if there are 100 religions in the world, at least 99 of them must be wrong," I sometimes argue with him. "They might all be a little bit right," I suggest. But mostly, unless they've heard something dead wrong about Wicca, we don't talk about religion. They do send me clippings of the increasing number of articles about pagan religions, and ask me questions if anything in those articles is unclear to them. But we don't talk down-home and personal much.

This is sad, as I have always been religious. I have always felt called to "the ministry," although until I found

Wicca, I did not know how to answer that call. Talking about religious ideas has been one of my greatest pleasures in life, and it is deeply disappointing to me that I cannot share this pleasure with my parents, who contributed more than they will ever know or believe they did.

Most of us who can't share our Witchcraft with our families would like to do so. Those of us for whom patient persistence is not a solution feel this as a loss of nurturing, and need to grieve for it. In *Toxic Parents*, authors Susan Forward and Craig Buck suggest a funeral for our expectations that our parents won't ever meet for us. It's a very powerful ritual, one that a solitary Witch or covener could easily adapt, and it makes the point very forcefully that we need to give ourselves a re-birth from such relationships.

As we deal with our parents' varying degrees of reluctance to accept Wicca as our faith, so must we anticipate the possibility of our children embracing a different religion when they are grown. I fantasize that the Explorer will marry a nice Wiccan girl and raise bouncing Wiccan babies — but he might not.

That has to be okay. If it isn't, or you're not sure that it is, if you make jokes to hide your anxiety about your kids becoming Catholics or Baptists when they grow up, you need to focus on the way it feels when your parents are disrespectful of your faith, and of your own right to choose it.

My opinion is that finding out the truth about our parents' religion is why we left it, and that finding out the truth about ours is why our kids will stay. Any of us could one day be on the other end of "Oh, by the way, Mom and Dad . . . ," but it's not something I worry a lot about. No matter which end of it we draw, though, we need to keep in mind that *Love unto all beings* is Her law.

WICCA AT HOME

Nearly everything we do at home can be done with Wicca in mind. From rearranging a room to brushing hair, everything can be a spell. For those of us who didn't grow up Wiccan, it might seem strange, but with practice, it will feel more and more comfortable. And if we share what you might call mundane blessings with our children, it will be "second" nature to them.

Not long ago, we got a free-standing closet in which to hang our ritual robes and store chalices, crowns and other such tools. Of course we consecrated it before we put anything inside — but that's not all we did. Because I've always liked the idea of a private magical land behind unsuspected doors, I painted a fantasy landscape on the three inside walls and the floor!

I'm no artist, believe me — Faerie Moon has that talent. But I mixed some craft paints, the kind that come in little bitty plastic pots, with some left-over latex wall paint, and got a wide range of colors. I applied these colors, lightest first, with a sponge. Later, I used some glittery fabric paint (left over from the coven banner) to tuck a castle into the painted hills.

The closet is scented, too, with the smudge we used to purify it, and with the magical scents of favorite potpourris tucked into the corners. Our sense of smell is our most evocative, so if you decide to let one of your closets do double duty as the gateway to a magical land, make charms out of potpourris that remind you of the magic of your youth. I used one that conjures up my grandmother's house. One caution: if you use veils with any of your robes, don't put them in while the scents are their strongest. Heavy scents

With salt and water in the names of Cerridwen and Llyr, the Explorer purifies the Quarters of his family's permanent backyard circle.

give some people severe headaches, and because veils cover our faces, the effect can be quite distracting.

The outer face of our closet's doors is decorated with a painted pentagram two feet in diameter. When I find the appropriate symbols, I will affix them at the points so that we can use that pentagram in meditations. (I particularly like Starhawk's pentagram meditations, and I'm searching for just the right symbols of them to paint and attach to the closet doors.)

You may need or prefer to be more subtle, but a small or hidden pentagram traced in paint or even in oil on the inside of a closet wall will bless it just as surely as a big shiny one!

We first used the following *Ritual of Space Dedication* to consecrate our back yard ramada several years ago. One thing we know now is that it's a good idea to make more than one charm if you're using a fabric pouch and planning to hang it outside: our lovingly embroidered felt pouch recently disintegrated! Of course, this ritual can be adapted for any room or patio, a bed, or even for a vehicle.

Ritual for Space Dedication

You will need a bowl of salt and a bowl of water, four candles in your quarter colors, a staff or a wand, incense and a burner, and a fifth candle of an energetic color.

If you are out of doors and it is possible, don't contain the candles, but allow their wax to imbue the ground. If this is not possible, try to set the candles in a container from which you can recover the melted wax to put bits from each candle into a charm which can remain in the space.

Water is purified and salt is blessed.

A staff or wand is held over the altar. Say:

> *May this altar and this place to all its corners be purified. In the name of Life and Death, so mote it be.*

All repeat:

> *So mote it be.*

Standing in the Goddess position in the center of the space to be dedicated, say;

> *Blessed be, thou creature of art!*

Raise incense to the East. Say:

> *May you be charged with the power of Air, and be strong and safe in the East, between the worlds and in all the worlds.*

Raise a candle to the South. Say:

> *May you be charged with the power of Fire, and be strong and safe in the South, in all the worlds and between the worlds.*

Raise the bowl of water to the West. Say:

*May you be charged with the power of Water, and
be safe and strong in the West, between the worlds
and in all the worlds.*

Raise the bowl of salt to the North. Say:

*May you be charged with the power of the Earth,
and be strong and safe in the North, in all the
worlds and between the worlds.*

Standing in the Goddess position in the center and circling
slowly (deosil) in place, say:

*May you be charged from the center above and
below, throughout and about, within and without.
May spirit be cherished here; may you stand with
strength and in safety, to be a haven between the
worlds and in all the worlds.*

Thank the Directions and the Goddess and God for
making this a "safe and nice place to be." Close the Circle
and let the corner candles burn down, if possible. Otherwise, save them and use them as Quarter candles until
they're gone.

In this ritual, we placed appropriately colored candles
in the corners of the room, area, or vehicle, orienting them
not at but as near as the corners come to the directions. By
doing this, the space we're consecrating is magically
aligned with the directions; we felt that if we put the
North candle, for instance, in the middle of a wall, the
space would be askew between the Worlds.

An ordinary barred security door becomes a magical gate when it is decorated with Celtic runes and a variety of designs stencilled with masking tape and bright enamel colors.

We used a staff because, for us, a staff represents adventure, and the spirit of adventure is very much at the core of our Witchcraft. Blessing and consecrating a space with a staff means to us that whenever we enter that place, we are on an adventure, and that puts us between the worlds whether we've cast a Circle formally or not.

Since we dedicated our ramada with this ritual, it often feels to me like a sort of magic carpet, even though it has an adobe floor. I often have visions of the whole henge, including the gardens and the pond at the west (fish and fountain and all!) transported to some magical land of adventure. I am always half-surprised to find the same old kitchen inside the screen door after all.

Here's another idea you may be able to use whole, or adapt. The sliding door to our back yard is covered with a wrought-iron barred security door. It's not as prison-like as it sounds, but it was pretty ugly. There was no way to make it less blatant, either, so we chose to see its boldness as a strength. Let's make it a <u>metaphysical</u> gate, too, we thought.

Using fairly inexpensive enamel paint from a do-it-yourself store and masking tape stencils cut with an Exacto knife, you too can make a security door into a work of art! It might take more than one weekend, but you can cover the door with runes and all kinds of designs — fish, cats, moons and stars, rolling hills, silhouettes of castles, wizards, whatever you like.

You do have to be careful not to get paint on anything else — yourself or your plants, for instance. But if you use an old sheet to cover everything, then you've got a delicately colored field from which you can go on to make many festive banners — two projects for the effort of one!

Our Gate is so obviously "decorative" that most people just admire the bright colors (which fit right in with the bright Mexican influences here) and never notice the religious symbols. The neighborhood kids have pronounced it "funky." A success all around, we think, so if anything like this appeals to you, go for it!

Spell for Transforming Anger

Sometimes something happens, to you or to somebody else, that makes you mad. Maybe a friend's husband beat her up, maybe a kid got detention at school for something s/he didn't do, maybe your candidate lost the election because of mud-slinging, maybe your car stereo got ripped off. Whatever it is, you are angry!

When it's something that you can't deal with directly, when the wife-beater's out on bail or the unfair teacher's tenured, when the politician can't be impeached for sleazy campaigning or the car stereo's already sold for quick cash, your anger has to be directed creatively or it'll do somebody harm.

I've used this spell a number of times. The words vary each time according to the specific situation. Sometimes I do parts of it in my head, when I can't contain my anger until I'm home and can cast a Circle. If you *are* able to cast a Circle, you'll need your Quarter candles and a center candle, and appropriate incense. Unless there's a reason to use something else, I like *Hecate* for this work.

As you light your Quarter candles, invoke the Guardians of each element.

Call upon the Guardian of Air to clear your mind of vengeful thoughts, to clarify your perspective.

Call upon the Guardian of Fire to temper your fierce anger with determination and to help you control your will.

Call upon the Guardian of Water to keep you from drowning in the tide of anger, to remind you that love is Her will and the greatest magic.

Call upon the Guardian of Earth to ground you, to connect you with firm strength and to steady you.

As you light the incense, affirm your transportation to a space between the worlds where you can be calm and direct your energies helpfully. Take as much time and as many deep breaths as you need here to ground and center. If your anger is very great, do not proceed until you stop shaking or crying!

As you light the center candle, invoke the appropriate aspects of the Goddess and the God.

Ask the Goddess to take the energy of your anger, transform it, and send it to the injured party to use in healing or as a shield, or to the injuring party to revive his or her conscience.

Ask the God to guide the energy of your anger and direct it toward the people involved, to strengthen them, or strengthen their awareness.

Ask the Goddess to transform what is left of your anger into a calm understanding that love unto all beings is Her law. Ask the God to transform what is left of your anger into a calm understanding that the Threefold Law is a lesson to be learned, not a vengeance to be delivered.

When the incense has burned away, extinguish the Quarter candles with thanks to the Guardians for their help. If possible, leave the center candle burning until it extinguishes itself.

In the meantime, get yourself something to eat and drink, blessing it first in your usual way. As you eat and drink, ask aloud to be nourished with love and trust. Say aloud that as the Goddess and the God give you the nourishment you now take in, so you give your energy to the God/dess to nourish the people you have just worked for.

When these things are done, try to give yourself a few minutes of quiet time. If you feel that it is appropriate, write to the person you have worked for and let them know that you have sent your energy to use as a shield against fear or guilt or injustice.

Very young children probably cannot do this work. They can, however, raise some pretty hefty angers, and it's important that they have a way to deal with it. A very simple version of this ritual that young children can do — with supervision, of course — is this:

Stand in the middle of a circle around which a grown-up has lit the Quarter candles. Say what makes you mad. Say how mad it makes you. Stomp up and down in the center of the circle and shout. When the energy level is high, fall to the ground and press your palms firmly against the floor.

Let your anger leave your body through your palms. Let it go into the floor, and through the floor, into the Earth underneath. This gives the energy of the anger back to the Mother.

Before you get up, say what you want to have happen. ("I want Billy to say he's sorry," or "I want the teacher to take my name off the board," or "I want Daddy not to work late," etc.)

Say how you would like to feel. ("I would like to feel calm," or "I would like to feel like going to the party," or "I would like Susan to be well," etc.) Then say:

> *I give my anger to Mother Earth so that She can send its energy to _____ and let it help.*

The whole ritual, including incense and food, should be supervised by an adult who does not participate. Children need to learn responsibility for their feelings, and this will help. Of course, a grown-up could use this same ritual in any situation that is too angry for rational direction of energy. We all want to have a tantrum sometimes, and this is much more constructive than breaking dishes!

3

Raising Children
to the Craft

Some Wiccan parents are reluctant to raise their children to the Craft, or even to teach their children anything about Wicca. Some families live where it's dangerous to be known as Wiccan, and the centuries of secrecy that kept Witchcraft alive seem to be a sensible precedent. Some Wiccans were educated so cruelly to their parents' religion that they are alarmed by the idea of teaching religion to their children. This experience sometimes generates the argument that it's "wrong to force my religion down my kid's throat. S/he should be free to make a choice when s/he grows up."

One of our questions about that is whether any uninformed choice is free. Another is what our children will learn about relationships if we shut them out or keep secrets. These parents, we think, need to reconsider: you don't have to teach Wicca to your kids the same way your parents' religion was taught to you!

Our neighborhood is predominantly Gospel Baptist. The Explorer's friends have invited him to Sunday School on occasion, and we've always given our permission. In true and natural pagan style, he's always declined to go, because "you have to get up too early."

On their part, the kids who saw me making our coven banner pronounced it "neat" without batting an eye. Cauldrons, chalices, Quarter candles — an altar! — fill our house, and none of the Explorer's friends give any of it a second glance.

The Explorer's teachers and the school principal have known since he entered school that we are Wiccan. I've insisted that if Christian (in two languages!) and Jewish songs are sung at the Winter Holiday program, so should the pagan *Deck the Halls* be raised.

The grade school called it a *Christmas* program before we pointed out that there's more than one Winter holiday. I've given teachers packets of information to clarify my requests that the green-faced, warty-nosed decorations be taken off the classrooms' October bulletin boards. And the Explorer has never encountered any discrimination as a result.

A very long time ago, maybe even before he started school, an older kid taunted the Explorer about devil worship. The Explorer and two or three other children were playing in a friend's front yard a few doors down when the older boy rode by. When he stopped, the other children looked up long enough to say, "Nuh-uh," and then they ignored him.

Not quite as long ago, the Explorer took a phone call ('dancer was in the shower and I was on my way home from work) about a letter I'd written to the paper. The call was from a fundie who told the Explorer he was being raised in a bad religion and would go to Hell. By the time the caller hung up, the Explorer was in tears: it had occurred to him to hang up, but he was afraid he'd get in trouble for doing that to a grown-up. We set him straight about that right away!

Those are the only troubles the Explorer's ever had with people being aware that he's Wiccan. Our car is covered with bumper stickers, including WITCHES HEAL and others that make our faith obvious. Canyondancer and I both wear a pentagram ring, and my necklaces are frequently visible.

Conversations the neighbor kids overhear include words like "coven," "Witches," "Witchcraft," "Goddess," and so on. Our rituals are sometimes overheard by our over-the-fence or across-the-alley neighbors. And our house is still, even so, the gathering-place-of-choice for all the Explorer's friends, with their parents' blessings.

In some places there would be more trouble, but some troubles are over-anticipated, too. Things change — so keep your finger on the local pulse!

Unless you never speak to your kids and never do anything religiously different from your Christian family or neighbors, unless Wicca has not changed your life at all, you are raising your children to the Craft. The only question is whether you will do it with respect for your kids' intelligence and potential — or not.

SUN DAY SCHOOL

We are fortunate to have a fairly large and well-accepted Wiccan and pagan community here in Tucson. At the University of Arizona, Arizona Student Pagans meets twice a month during the school year, offering introductory classes to the public as well as to University students. And every couple of years, the HP and HPs of the oldest local mixed coven offer public classes under the title *The Basics of the Old Religion.*

Our family has taken this class twice. The first time, the Explorer was very young, and paid more attention to the interesting people taking the class than he did to the materials the instructors presented. The second time, though, he learned quite a bit.

If such classes are available where you live, we recommend them highly, for several reasons. Taking a class with Mom and Dad makes a kid feel pretty grown up. It also lets a kid know that Witchcraft is not just a family tradition, but something that's gone on for thousands of years, something that goes on all over the country and beyond.

Some of the material will be hard for children to understand, which gives you a chance to talk about the Craft in some depth and explain it in terms your kids can understand. The second time, the Explorer was particularly interested in reincarnation, and we had some really neat conversations about it.

Talking about these things gives you a basis for comparison: how are your family's traditions different from others, and how are they the same? Do all the Witches in your family believe exactly the same things, or are there interesting differences among family members or coveners?

When he realized the Explorer would be attending, the HP teaching our class asked me whether he should be concerned about the sexual references and the nudity pictured in some of the slides he shows. I reassured him that in the Wiccan context, sex and nudity are inoffensive, and this context is furthermore a vital counterbalance to the dominant social attitudes (which we'll explore later).

It's true that kids can be self-conscious about seeing pictures of a skyclad gathering and hearing grown-ups talk about sex. It is not true that their embarrassment or the pictures and discussions will do them any harm. Children have built-in defenses: they simply don't pay conscious attention to things they can't understand.

A child's unconscious attention follows parental cues, so if Mom and Dad respond calmly, with interest and agreement, then a child's subconscious will "file" those reactions with the images and information s/he may seem to be ignoring. Years later, when adolescents want to know what to think about their bodies (and other peoples'), and need to know what attitude to take toward sex and nudity, the mental support for reverent pleasure will be there.

Other useful concepts will be available, too; a wealth of information is available in classes like those we've been able to attend. If classes aren't available in your community (and if you can't organize them yourself), then consider introducing casual lessons, perhaps from a book like *Buckland's Complete Book of Witchcraft*.

It's not necessary to teach Wicca by rote, although there are some things we all like to memorize. It's far more appropriate to experience Witchcraft, to feel the wind against our faces, feel the fire at our backs. There are a lot of ways to bring a Wiccan education to our children, and we'll talk about some of them in the pages that follow. In the meantime, let's talk about those twin parental banes, video games and Saturday morning cartoons.

ELECTRONIC GAMES AND SATANIC CARTOONS

Five or ten years ago, a book like this one wouldn't have had paragraphs like the ones you're about to read: about Nintendo (and other video game systems), and the cartoons that some say are Satanic. Today, though, we need to talk about these things.

We've heard lots about the effects, good and bad, of video games on children. It was with mixed emotions that I heard armed forces generals affirming that jet pilots' performances are improved by their early practice on the game keyboard.

I don't think that dropping bombs is a good thing for young women and men to be doing. But improved eye-hand and eye-hand-brain coordination is good, and as long as video games don't become war training devices exclusively, I think it's worth the effort to make them the tools of our trade, too.

We bought the Explorer his first game set when he was five; he bought the Nintendo he has now with his own money, saved from holiday gifts and his allowance. He understood from the beginning that buying games was up to him. The Atari we bought him came with two; all the others he's ever owned he bought with his own money. To avoid spending all of it, he worked out trading deals with his friends, selling the games he had beaten and buying used ones for less than half-price. From this experience, he continues to learn how to budget his money.

Recently he was considering buying a Sega game-player, which has better graphics than his Nintendo — but it costs a fortune, and there are fewer games available for it. He weighed the advantages of better graphics against the disadvantages of cost and scarcity of games, considered the fact that still fewer of those fewer games are available to rent — and decided to stick with the system he's got now. No matter what decision he'd made, he learned a lot about value and how to make those "big-ticket purchase" decisions. He'll need that skill for the rest of his life.

As for the games themselves, yes, a lot of them involve killing an opponent. But most kids old enough to grasp the object of the game, understand the rules and powers of the "guys" on the screen, and coordinate the keyboards, are also old enough to distinguish between games and reality.

Many of the games are adventures loosely — very loosely, in some cases — based on Western mythologies. The "guys" our kids move on the screen have to earn their magical tools, anticipate and avoid dangers, and use their wits as well as their weapons to defeat the enemy.

These skills may not come in handy very often in mundane life, but these games introduce our children to magic's different logic, and help to lay a foundation for *real* mystical thought later on. Video games can teach kids something about cooperation, too — an attitude and skill helpful in both mundane and magical efforts.

In fact, for the kids we know, the time they spend playing games may be the only time they have a chance to hear peer congratulations and to be part of a winning team. When it's a chance for a kid to surpass the low expectations his parents and teachers have of him, and succeed in something that matters to him, it pretty much is a magical effort, mundane though the popcorn we clean up afterward may be.

Sometimes we have found the Explorer already familiar with a concept we want to teach him — through his games. The use of magical language, for instance; or the idea that roughly similar rules change slightly from ritual to ritual (game to game). We have also found "game reality" a useful source of analogy when we're trying to make points he might otherwise not understand.

I get sick of hearing the bleepity-blip of video games, sure. But when I see five or six ten- and eleven-year-old boys playing in teams, making next-step decisions by consensus, sharing hints and helping each other's "guys" stay alive, I'm going to *complain?* Not when I look out the window and see Bloods and Crips milling in the street like cattle, I'm not. Not when I still hear people arguing that it's everyone for themselves as far as food and shelter and medical care go, I'm not.

Video games aren't my choice for recreation, but I don't have to play them, either, and our children need to have the freedom to develop confidence in their own choices. I think we will be more successful at raising "good guys" if we respect their right to make different choices than we would. The Goddess' love is poured forth across the lands, and is manifest even in video games; I think that if Wiccan parents listen carefully, they will be able to hear Her voice even in the bleepity-blips.

As for cartoons, I'm sure you've chuckled as often as we have to hear Rainbow Brite and the Smurfs called Satanic; you may have rolled your eyes as you hear them chirping out from the television on Saturday morning. If your kids don't watch cartoons at your house, they probably catch them on somebody else's television at least once in a while. Like the fundies who abhor them, there's really no way to avoid them completely.

We share a national concern that the violence riddling many cartoons desensitizes our kids and substitutes a dangerous unreality for the truth of assault. The Explorer has never watched the shows that overtly glamorize combat, and he's never bought the play figures that go with those cartoons. (He's found a GI Joe figure or two, however; usually with an arm or a leg amputated. I think it's fitting that the very few war dolls he has are maimed.)

Problems are present even with the best cartoons, of course. The Smurfs are of necessity patriarchal; there are one hundred males and only one female! But Mother Nature is their patron, they do careful magic in self-defense, and their only enemy is an incarnation of greed and exploitation. The Explorer hasn't watched that show in several years — but when he did, the cats enjoyed it too, and played with a couple of stuffed Smurfs we got from the thrift shop.

He-Man was a favorite for a long time. (None of us think much of the new show, though.) The parallels to our pagan worldview were often useful. Although male characters dominated the show, the few females were their equals, and later She-ra got her own show. The Explorer appreciated the moral points He-Man made at the end of every half-hour, and so did we.

Because these shows were not set in the real world, the fighting he saw in them did not seem, to the Explorer, to be modeling real-world behavior. Other cartoons purport to take place in the same world we inhabit, and I think the violence they include is confusing. Even so, my worry was never that the Explorer would be misinformed about firearms or flamethrowers, but that he would accept the relationships those shows posit.

Not only are personal relationships poorly modeled in most cartoons — not to mention other "kid shows" —

but the relationships among social classes, between governments, among citizens and governments, and the relationships of civilization (using the term loosely) and nature are also unrealistically presented.

The Explorer sometimes watches *Captain Planet* now, though not regularly. The little I've seen of it — an international team of young characters, each contributing an elemental power bestowed by Gaia for the as-needed creation of the title's super-hero — looks and sounds wonderful.

One must expect most cartoons to be one-dimensional, of course, like any other half-hour or hour-long television show that exists primarily to make money for its sponsors. Cartoons aren't any worse than 90% of the live-action shows broadcast. It's just that they're more often watched without supervision, so that their subtle fictions go unchallenged. Like your children are, or will be, the Explorer is able to notice that real families are different from television families. But the premises in cartoons are disguised in animated fantasy landscapes, and sneak into the subconscious minds of children who aren't yet "hip."

We don't think that a ban on television is a reasonable solution, although some families do. We figure that banning television, or setting arbitrary time limits on watching, is as much a cop-out as letting kids watch anything they want. A moderate course, though it takes more time and effort, seems more responsible to us.

Watch what your kids are watching. Not all the time, of course, but know what shows they like to see, and if you have objections, tell your kids why. Even if the kid is too young to understand your explanation, explain anyway. If what you're saying doesn't register, the fact that you *are* explaining eventually will, and you won't have established a pattern of overpowering your kids just because you're bigger or louder.

Remember, too, that kids have different tastes than adults do, and that kids of different ages like different things. Each of our children is an individual: what frightens his friends may just seem silly to the Explorer; what they think is "cool" may look atrocious to him. From the black-and-white television in our bedroom we can often hear the laugh track of *America's Funniest People* over the pauses of whatever we're watching on PBS, and that's okay.

It's okay that your children like to watch different things, and read different things, and listen to different music, and eat different foods than you do, *as long as you know what they're doing* and know that it isn't hurting them. Take the time to watch the shows they like with them now and then, and take the time to talk about those shows. Try to appreciate the shows from a kid's point of view, if you expect a kid to appreciate your opinion.

Of course, neither video games nor television shows, cartoon or live-action, can be allowed to get in the way of real life. Meal times and bed times and homework and playing outside and family activities are all more important.

Be sure that those things are available to your kid, and be sure that you take responsibility for them. It is unrealistic to expect a child to remember to break for dinner or to end an exciting game to go to bed; and if we keep the television on for news while we're at the table, a kid's going to think it's just as reasonable to keep it on for something s/he likes to watch.

Even the worst shows can spark interesting family discussions, as long as we don't take our kids' choice of entertainment personally. Remember, senses of humor change! Kids watch some shows to have something in common with their friends, and we'd rather have the Explorer watch a couple of stupid shows — which we can talk about — than do some of the things kids do to feel like they're part of a group. We can ask:

> "What would happen if a kid really did that
> in school?"
> "How would it feel if one of your friends played
> that joke?"
> "Have you been to a house that looks like that?"
> "I wonder how much money clothes like that cost?"
> "Have you ever seen anyone get shot? Let's watch
> the news and see if we can figure out what that
> would be like."

If we are sensitive to our children's developmental needs, we'll be able to help our kids meet those needs in healthy and creative ways. Kids need to know themselves as individuals, separate from their parents and on the way to independent adulthood, and they need to check out what other people's attitudes are like. We need to support them in this quest, even if it means sitting through *The Cosby Show* one more time!

Finally, a word about those Teenage Mutant Ninja Turtles. I took the Explorer and one of his friends to the first movie in the series, he's seen it at the theater with another friend's family, and we've also rented it a couple of times — fortunately, I kind of like it. One thing I like quite a lot about it is that it's pretty well pagan!

Say what? Say martial arts! The martial arts originated long ago in countries that were then — and are still, to some extent — pagan. They are not founded in the idea that our strengths are "God-given," but in the idea that self-discipline leads to enormous inner power.

In the first movie, The Turtles' teacher, who has been kidnapped, appears to the Turtles as they are fire-gazing. He assuages their anguish by reminding them that their real power lies not in control of their bodies, but in their control of their minds. *Amen,* if you'll pardon my language!

So, when the shows your kids watch and the video games they play drive you up a wall, remember Splinter's caution. Remember too that WE ARE GOD/DESS, and make an effort to show your children the faces of the Gods — no matter what it is they're watching!

SYMBOL AND METAPHOR

The Explorer has not yet memorized the Charge or the Rune or all our Quarter calls, but all of our liturgical material is familiar to him. He's been reciting bits in Circle for years. He knows a few chants, and he knows what to expect of Sabbats and Esbats, whether we do them in the privacy of our own 'stead or in the park together with others, solitaires and coveners alike.

Children develop the capacity for symbolic thought — *metaphor* — somewhere between the ages of eight and eleven. It's not beyond a child of that age to understand that no, there isn't a big Lady in the sky, but that the spirit of life is like a mother to everything.

The Explorer's first models for the Goddess and God were Mother Nature and Father Time. Father Time is not a strictly Wiccan figure, but he embodies the ideas of mortality and natural cycles, and he is a non-threatening figure in the cowan world. Though most of Wicca's rituals emphasize the God's youthful aspects, it's important to remember that the Sage is also God-like. Men do not all die in their prime, and we need male as well as female role models for our elder-hoods.

The Wiccan world view has developed over thousands of years from uncountable personal experiences, so it makes sense to us to explain Wicca and the world in terms of our personal experience. Here's an example of what I mean:

When the Explorer was about four years old, we went early to a site to see the city's Fourth of July fireworks. While we were waiting for the main display, he spotted a few back-yard fireworks, bottle rockets mostly, shooting into the deepening dusk. He thought those wobbly red streaks were what we'd come to see. We told him that they were nothing to what would start in a few minutes, and when the city finally did fire it all, the child was absolutely amazed.

The next summer we went to Disneyland and told the Explorer about Disneyland's Electrical Parade and fireworks. "Disneyland will make the Fourth of July look like back-yard fireworks," we said. He couldn't imagine what the Disneyland fireworks would be like, but he could understand the metaphor. He wasn't disappointed, either.

Now, years later, we can compare anticipated experiences to things we've already done using the fireworks example, and even when what we anticipate is quite beyond his capacity to imagine, he can get some idea what to expect. We tell him that Life makes Disneyland look like back-yard fireworks — and we don't think he'll ever be disappointed with that expectation.

To tell you the truth, we think that the Summerland, that experience beyond death, will be something like the Disneyland fireworks, too — and we haven't been disappointed yet.

WHAT'S THE YOUNGER GENERATION COMING TO?

The Explorer's friends share lots of "information" about the ways of the world and the ways of the human body. Taking even the most impossible religious legends to be literally true, many of these children have some trouble distinguishing fact from fiction; the Explorer makes his own evaluations and then shares them with us.

He is old enough now that he can draw on his own experiences in answer to many of his questions about other religions, and about the conclusions his friends draw from their dogma. (Of course, we've been explaining the world to him in terms of his own experience, too, same as you're doing with your kids.)

The Explorer understands that all religions are trying to answer the same questions he's asking. He accepts that every religion phrases its questions and its answers differently. So far, he finds that Wicca speaks most clearly to him, in best harmony with his own observation and experience.

We think it's really important for Wiccan parents to give their children the opportunity to compare personal experience to thealogy and draw their own conclusions. This is the most appropriate way to teach the Craft; and after all, that's how most of us came to Wicca, isn't it?

Children can be grounded in Wicca very gently. Notice how good the bath water feels at the end of the day; make it feel better with herbs. Notice how good it feels to take a deep breath when you watch the sunrise. See how a candle or a crackling fire is hot and bright like the Sun. Aren't rocks strong like mountains, maybe the northern mountains? Isn't it cozy and safe under the bedcovers, dark like a cave deep in the Earth?

Isn't it neat that sometimes when you're thinking about somebody, they call or you get a letter from them? Or that sometimes when you want something special for dinner, you come home and that very thing is almost ready?

The Goddess gives abundant opportunities to lay a humanist foundation upon which our children can build a Wiccan faith. What stands out in our experience as different from what we learned can be what our children are taught; their norm. Blessing the bread at dinner. Libations. Quarter candles. Attention to the phases of the Moon and Sun.

Recycling and other environmentally sensitive habits. Respect for other cultures. Lateral thinking and consensus decision-making. Attention to passage through life's stages — birth, puberty, adulthood, etc. Appreciation of religious and cultural differences. The common ground of community involvement. Respect for each other's feelings.

There are a number of very good books about raising children. We are not talking about books that tell us what to do, although most good ones give helpful examples. We're talking about books that give us the kind of information we need to decide what to do in various situations.

We need to know how, and in what stages, human brains develop from infancy. We need to know which developmental skills are indications of readiness for what sorts of experiences. We need to understand the ways that children of various ages are likely to express certain needs so that we don't misinterpret their behavior.

When we were pregnant, 'dancer and I read all the books we could get, and believe me, we took a lot of ribbing from our friends. "Are you going to raise the baby by the book?" they'd ask snidely. "Parenting is just natural," they'd say, and add, "kids aren't machines."

No, they're not. But they aren't miniature adults, either; the developmental stages they go through are both delicate and critical. *Homecoming* is a book John Bradshaw wouldn't have needed to write if raising kids were a cinch. It's about healing, "reclaiming and championing" your wounded inner child. Our inner children — Starhawk says "younger self," Jung says "wonder child" — are wounded by ignorance and insensitivity to basic developmental needs.

Some of the books that we've found very helpful are listed here, but this isn't a comprehensive list. It doesn't even include all the books we read and relied upon, because we've cleaned our bookshelves since the Explorer was born. But they *are* books we recommend as being useful and compatible with Wicca.

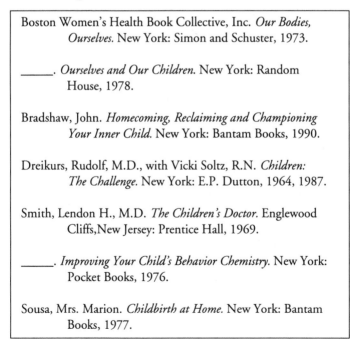

Boston Women's Health Book Collective, Inc. *Our Bodies, Ourselves.* New York: Simon and Schuster, 1973.

_____. *Ourselves and Our Children.* New York: Random House, 1978.

Bradshaw, John. *Homecoming, Reclaiming and Championing Your Inner Child.* New York: Bantam Books, 1990.

Dreikurs, Rudolf, M.D., with Vicki Soltz, R.N. *Children: The Challenge.* New York: E.P. Dutton, 1964, 1987.

Smith, Lendon H., M.D. *The Children's Doctor.* Englewood Cliffs,New Jersey: Prentice Hall, 1969.

_____. *Improving Your Child's Behavior Chemistry.* New York: Pocket Books, 1976.

Sousa, Mrs. Marion. *Childbirth at Home.* New York: Bantam Books, 1977.

Remember when any of these books says that "magic" or "magical thinking" is pretend, superstitious, etc., they're talking about *fairy-tale magic,* not what we do; don't let it turn you off. Kids are more important than petty semantics.

Some Projects for the Family

A great way to teach Wicca gently and to demonstrate Wiccan respect for the family unit, is to work on projects together. Most Wiccan families are already recycling everything from aluminum and glass, to the clothes we give to (and buy from!) our local thrift shops. Many of us are already participating in local environmental efforts — in Tucson, we've been planting trees.

Some of us are politically active and our children march or help at mailing parties with us. Some of us are able to circle publically, too. All of these activities are wonderful family experiences, but even those of us who are publically inclined and "out of the broom closet" like to do some family things together at home. Here are some ideas we like.

Calendars! Everybody needs one. One of Tucson's High Priests makes them for his friends with drawings he has collected over the years. Any of us can illustrate wall or desk calendars, and pocket cards with future dates are easily available. At relatively little expense, your local fast-printer can pad your calendars or give them a spiral binding.

Another calendar that's lots of fun to make is an *advent calendar.* Most of us associate advent calendars with the days leading up to Christmas, but we can make them for our own holidays, too. Between any two Sabbats, for instance, it's fun to open the "little paper doors."

We open one between Mabon and Samhain. Outwardly, it's a steaming cauldron; under the doors are all kinds of pagan images. For the longer periods of time pagan advent calendars cover, you might use paper larger than standard notebook size.

Collect several pictures, drawing them yourself or clipping them from newspapers and magazines (and even from the richly illustrated advertisements for books and magazines that come in the mail). You'll need one for every day on the advent calendar.

If young children want to contribute their art, try making your calendar on poster board. Someone old enough to use an Exacto knife will need to do the cutting, but poster boards are both big enough to take the larger drawings children make and sturdy enough to last several years.

When you have enough pictures, decide on art for the front of the calendar. Draw it colorfully on paper the same size as the page or poster board that will hold all the pictures, and be sure to leave lots of room to cut the flaps that will hide the pictures. Finally, arrange the pictures on the backer to match the pattern of windows on the cover sheet, and glue the pictures down. Be sure they are completely dry before you assemble the calendar. Then, after you've cut each window on three sides so that it can be folded open, glue the cover drawing onto the page with the pictures.

Use a very thin line of glue at the outer edge of the cover page, or you might accidentally obscure a picture. If you aren't using poster board, you'll need to mount the calendar on stiff cardboard. We use picture-frame backs, the kind that have built-in tripods, so we can set the finished calendar up on a shelf.

Trimmed with ribbon or glitter or even shells or pretty stones, these calendars can last for years and become favorite holiday decorations. At the same time, they teach our family to focus on Witchcraft's symbols, anticipate

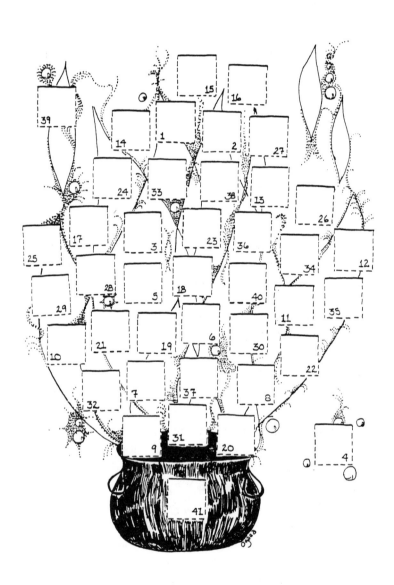

Advent Calendar

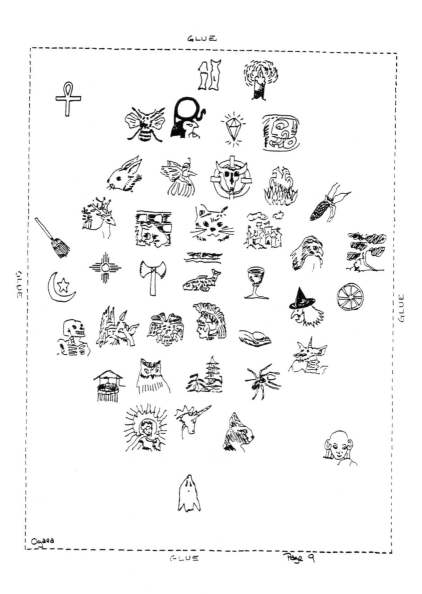

Advent Calendar

Wiccan holidays, and remind us of the common ground we share with other pagan faiths.

Coloring books are fun to make, too. Drawing pictures of Sabbat and Esbat celebrations is a cozy way to fill up rainy hours if puddle-stomping isn't practical.

If you want to use them as gifts, you can photocopy the original pictures, stack them in order with cardboard backers and construction paper covers separating the sets, and have them padded at the local copy shop. Once that's done, it's easy to separate the individual coloring books.

Of course, if you want to draw enough original pictures for several coloring books, that's great, too. Depending on how specifically Wiccan your pictures are, these coloring books make nice donations to local children's shelters and hospitals. Wrapped in tissue paper with a small box of crayons, they're hours of fun.

Brooms can be made in a variety of ways. You can look for straight, slender fallen branches and tie a collection of stiff twigs to one end, or you can make one with — yea verily, construction paper. Use a tightly rolled tube for the handle of the broom. Wind a shorter piece around one end, and cut "fringe" for the besom. (You can even use it to sweep your project scraps off the table!)

Banners much less complicated than what you'd make for a coven are easy to make with glue, scissors and a package of construction paper. Family coats-of-arms are fun to make, and fun to design if you don't know what yours looks like. Sabbat and Esbat coats-of-arms make wonderful decorations, too.

Greeting cards, very expensive in the stores, can also be handmade. You can make them fancy, of course, but you can make them folksy, too, with little more than scissors, glue — and the ever-popular construction paper.

Stickers from the craft or stationery store, doilies sold for Valentines, ribbon scraps, glitter, sequins, markers, crayons, confetti — all these things and more will personalize the cards and stationery you can design and make.

Your local fast printing shop will have stiff paper on which you can have a design printed several times to make post cards, and you can personalize each one. Stationery is easy to make too — just be sure to leave enough room to write a letter! The cost of printing it at the photocopier's saves a lot of money over the cost of commercial sets.

What else can families get together to make? Well, with knitted, crocheted or tatted doilies (that you make yourself or find at a thrift shop) and a length of ribbon or cord, you can make gathered pouches. These don't require any other materials, although a large safety pin (diaper pins work especially well) attached to the end of the ribbon makes it easier to thread through the edge of the doilies.

If you enjoy hand sewing or have a machine, you can make fabric pouches. An advantage to these is that you can cut them to shape. Faerie Moon and I have found light-weight leather scraps in a variety of colors and smallish pieces of rabbit fur at a shop that sells fabric by weight, and these would make very nice pouches, too. *(See Rite or Wrong?)*

Something families can always do together is play games. For instance, we can play word games with our kids almost anywhere; in the car, on a hike, in a waiting room.

I'm Going to the Moon is an old favorite of ours. It's an alphabet game, and it can be played as a *Wiccan* alphabet game very easily. Here's how it might sound:

The first player begins it by saying, "I'm going to the Moon, and I'm taking . . . an athame."

The second player continues: "I'm going to the Moon, and I'm taking an athame and . . . a bolline."

The next player goes on: "I'm going to the Moon, and I'm taking an athame, a bolline, and . . . a censor."

Each player repeats the growing list of luggage and adds an item (or a person) that begins with the next letter of the alphabet. For each game you can assign a theme — Witches' tools, magical places, magical beasts, etc.

My Grandfather's Cat is another alphabet game, a little more complicated than *I'm Going to the Moon.* The first player says, "My grandfather's cat is an *awful* cat who *acts arrogant.*" The next player doesn't have to remember any of the "a" words, but describes the cat with "b" words. In each description, there has to be an adjective and a noun; the third word can be an adjective, a noun, an adverb, or another verb.

"My grandfather's cat is a *finicky* cat who *flies* and *feasts,*" you might say, or perhaps your grandfather's cat is a *wonderful* cat who *waves* a *wand.* You might even want to talk about your grand<u>mother's</u> cat, or the High Priestess' cat!

If your family enjoys board games, and the kids are old enough, try Witches' Scrabble®. It follows the same rules as the standard game, but you keep the words you spell relevant to the Craft, or a particular Sabbat, or another theme.

Now and again, in a cowan catalogue, you find games that are almost Wiccan. There are several sources for cooperative card games and board games. (*See Appendix C.*) Some Tarot decks include instructions for games, and encouraging a child to tell stories about the images on the cards, even before s/he learns their traditional interpretations, will be fun for everybody.

4

Magic

Magic at its most basic is energy collected from life's reservoir, raised, and directed toward a goal. Wiccans work magic in particular ways, with certain words and gestures, because over our generations those forms have acquired the power of our understandings-in-common. There are at least as many ways of working magic as there are cultures and religions in the world. Wicca doesn't use all of them, but Wiccans can use almost any!

Formal Witchcraft — full Circles, ancient forms, precise liturgies — raises power through adults' minds. Children who are not yet familiar with or "fluent in" the cultural sources of Craft rituals don't draw the same strength from them. But magic has been in the world longer than even our oldest consolidated customs, and children can bring their energy to magical work even if they don't work like adults. Don't discourage your kids from raising and directing energy just because they can't use the same forms you do.

Within Wicca's basic symbolic framework *(see Appendix B)*, let your children make their own magic. You'll be able to introduce them to the formalities later; when they're young, it's more important to develop their confidence and to integrate magical work into their lives so that it doesn't seem unreasonable to them later.

As soon as your child is old enough to manage the concentration, you can give her some visualization exercises. Work with the child's natural inclination and to validate his own experience. In early exercises, let the child choose the image s/he wishes to visualize.

Guided meditations are good for children. If you can't find or afford an appropriate one in a local occult shop or in the catalogues, make your own. Write your own empowering script slowly, describing places your child knows and loves.

Choose some soothing music and read your script into a tape recorder while the music fills the background. Turn the music up higher than you would for conversation; your voice will dominate the recording because you'll be much closer to the microphone than the music is.

The Cave of Many Colors
A Guided Meditation by Ashleen O'Gaea

Imagine yourself lying on a soft, fresh-smelling grassy place in a quiet, sunny wood. The sun is bright and golden, shining through the green, rustling leaves. Feel the gentle wind touch your face, softly, like Mother's fingers. Relax. Relax your whole body. Just relax, just let go, trust the Earth. You are comfortable lying on the grassy forest floor. Just relax. See the patterns the sun makes in the branches above, and just relax. Smell the earth, smell the trees, feel the wind, feel the sunshine and the shadows, and just relax.

Let yourself sink deeply into the soft grass, let it hold you. Feel it beneath you, feel it cradling you, and just relax. Feel it hold you. Trust the Earth and just relax. The sun is warm, the breeze is gentle, the grassy ground holds you and you are very comfortable.

Feel the grassy ground beneath you. Feel it under your heels, under your ankles and calves. Feel the Earth, safe and secure, holding you like your mother, holding you, cradling you like the womb. Feel it holding your hips, your back, your shoulders, your neck. Feel the Earth support your hands and your wrists and your elbows and your arms. Feel the Earth support you and just relax, relax. Just relax and enjoy yourself. Feel good.

You are supported, you are embraced. You are relaxed, you are safe and secure. You are lying in a beautiful, soft, sunny, grassy forest clearing, blue sky above you. The sun is shining softly through the branches. You're safe and comfortable, and you have no cares, no worries. Just lie and enjoy the comfort, feeling the wind and smelling the grass and the leaves.

Feel the sun on your face, hear the wind in the trees. Feel the grass beneath you, the coolness and moisture. Hear the birds singing. Hear them rustling on the forest floor. Listen to the squirrels running through the branches above you. Listen for the woodpeckers and the hummingbirds. Just relax and be aware of this place, relax and be right in the middle of this clearing, safe and quiet and comfortable.

(Pause)

It's such a nice clearing, such a beautiful place, so warm, so full of sound and smell and color and life. You're very comfortable, very safe and secure, very relaxed. And now, with no effort at all, you rise up and move, as fast or slow as you like, across the clearing. You move easily across the clearing to a place where the woods meet the edge of some rocky foothills. And hidden among the rocks, you find a small, secret cave.

This is your cave, yours alone. No one else has ever seen it, no one else knows it's here or what it looks like. It's yours alone, and it's a safe cave that pleases you. You look inside the cave, feel the breeze coming from it, and you see a shaft of sunlight coming down between the rocks that make the ceiling of the cave.

This sunlight is warm and peaceful, and it is your sunlight. The secret cave with its earthy floor and the beautiful shaft of sunlight is yours, yours alone, quiet and peaceful and safe; a special, secret place.

You step inside the cave, and it is dark and cool, and you feel at home here. The sunlight coming through the roof is like a golden rainbow. It is warm and beautiful and you want to touch it, to feel it. You step forward and you are standing in the shaft of sunlight. You can feel the warm sun on your face, and the light makes you squint. You feel alive, tingling with life, and you are safe, and you are relaxed and comfortable.

You are alert, and you notice every detail of your cave. The dusty floor is almost white where the sunlight touches it. You can see the dust dancing, swirling upward in the warm sunlight. The bits of dust sparkle like diamonds against the dim walls of the cave.

You reach out and touch the dark, cool walls. The palms of your hands caress the stone. Feel the rock beneath your fingers. Feel its texture, the cracks and mosses. Feel the curving rocks, feel how solid they are. Lean against the walls. You are safe here, safe and comfortable and relaxed.

Stand in the shaft of sunlight, and see it light your hands as you hold them up to the light. Move your hands in the light, watch the dance of light and shadow on your hands, feel it on your skin. Close your eyes and turn your face up toward the light, and feel it touch you. Feel the light stroke your face, feel the sunlight. Your hands are still dancing in the light. Watch them, and see that the light is turning red. See all the different colors of red that there are, see them dance on your skin, feel them. Feel the red touch you.

Red is life, red is love, red is safe and secure. Red is the color of blood, and you can feel the blood in your body. You can feel your heartbeat in this red light, feel it pumping life through your body. Feel the strength of life, and see its beauty in the red light.

(Pause)

See the light change to orange, and feel the orange light on your hands. See all the different colors of orange that dance on your skin, feel the orange colors within you, feel them all through your body. Feel the orange all around you, feel it in the walls of the cave, feel it all over.

(Pause)

Watch the sunlight turn to yellow, bright yellow. Feel yellow touch your skin, see all its different colors. Feel yellow's energy dance within it. See it on the walls, feel it in the air. See the dust dance in the yellow light. Feel your hands dancing in the yellow light. Let it cover you, let it embrace you, let it warm you. Breathe it in.

(Pause)

And now the light changes and is green, light green at first, like spring. Feel all the different colors of green in the light, from the palest green to the darkest, deepest green. Feel them all, feel them on your skin. See them, see them on your hands. See all the greens on the walls of your cave. Feel them through your body. Taste them. Let your whole self be green with the light.

(Pause)

The light will change to blue now, to all the colors of blue. Feel them. Feel them on your skin, see them. Dance in the blue light. Drink it in, let the blue light remind you of water. Notice all the colors of blue on the walls of your cave. Notice all the colors of blue on your hands. Feel them all on your hands. Let your hands dance in the blue light. Let the blue light know everything about you, and let the beautiful blue light show you all of its colors.

(Pause)

The blue is getting darker now, and it's indigo. It's dark and rich and warm and it has many shades to it. Feel it all over you, feel it within you. See it on your skin, feel it on your skin. See indigo on the walls of the cave, see how it deepens the shadows. Feel it inside and outside, know that it is everywhere. It is soft and comfortable and strong. Relax with it, let it swirl around you.

(Pause)

And let the indigo light turn to violet now. The sunlight in your cave is violet now, all the colors of violet. Let them dance with your hands, these violet colors. Feel how soft they are. Feel how they trust you, the violet colors, feel how you trust them. See the violets on the wall of the cave, see them on your hands. See the violet light, and let it see you, inside and out. Breathe it, taste it, let it come in and out of you like breath.

(Pause)

And now let the light be sunny gold again, touching you and touching the walls of your cave. Let the dust dance in it again, just for you. Know that you have received a precious gift, know that these colors are yours now, forever and ever. Know that these colors have been given to you to keep inside, to know and to trust. Know that these colors are yours to see and feel whenever you want them. Remember how strong the colors are, and remember that you can use their strength, for they are yours now. They have been given to you in this very special cave. This experience is yours, all yours, and it is yours now and forever, whenever you need it. You have all the colors within you now. You are safe with them, and they are safe with you, and the secret of this cave is yours forever.

(Pause)

Look up now, through the crack in the top of the cave, and see that the sunlight has become moonlight, silvery and gentle. Feel it touch you softly, like a kitten. Feel it on your hands and face. Touch it, hold it in your hands. Feel the Moon and the stars glitter in the silvery light. Feel the cool, tingling touch of this light inside you. Breathe it in. It is yours. You can see the Moon and the stars through the roof of your cave. You can feel the cool, safe darkness and the sparkling of life all around you. You can feel the mysteries, you can touch them. You can breathe them and see them. You do not need to speak, for the Moon and the stars and the light of evening and midnight are deep within you now.

(Pause)

Lie down on the floor of your cave and enjoy this for as long as you would like. Feel the moonlight, feel how gently it touches you. Notice how safe and comfortable you feel with the moonlight beside you. Hear the sounds of the night, the birds, the clouds, the darkness. Close your eyes and enjoy this for a little while.

(Pause)

Open your eyes now, and see the cave in sunlight again. Feel the floor of the cave beneath you, and slowly, slowly rise up from it until you are standing again in the shaft of sunlight. This is magical light, it is all the light there is, Sun and Moon and stars and the light of life, and it is yours. It is strong light, and now its strength is yours. It will be yours forever, like this cave. Like this cave, you are magical, and you always will be. The magic of this cave lives within you now — be aware of that.

You will take the magic with you when you leave your cave. You are leaving now, but you are not sad, for its magic is with you, and you can come back to it whenever you want. It is your cave and your magic. You can come back to the forest clearing now, and the magic is still with you, and always will be. As you move, as quickly or as slowly as you want, back to the forest clearing, remember that the magic of the cave is with you. Remember that the cave and the magic are yours to keep, for ever and ever.

You are back in the forest clearing now, and it is quiet but for the wind and the birds and the squirrels. Hear them. Listen for their songs and their footsteps. Lie down on the forest floor and feel the strong Earth beneath you. Relax. The grassy forest floor is safe and strong and will hold you. The Earth is your Mother and She will hold you safely. You are safe and relaxed and comfortable here. Slowly, slowly, the grassy forest floor becomes your chair again. Now you can feel the arms of your chair. Now you can feel your feet on the floor.

(Pause)

You are still safe, you are still relaxed. In a moment, you will open your eyes and be in your house, safe and secure with people you love and who love you. When you open your eyes to home, you will wait for just a moment before you get up. And in that moment, you will remember the forest, you will remember the cave, you will remember the colors and the lights. You will remember the magic, and you will remember that it is yours, and you will know that it is within you now, for ever and ever.

(Pause)

And now you will get up, and you will be completely back at home. And deep within you, when you are very still and pay attention, you will still feel all the colors and all the magic. Blesséd be. I love you.

A meditation can take a child on a traditional journey, to a river bank, into a cave, through the clouds. Such a tape can take a child successfully through a test, to the solution of a problem with a friend, to a restoration of trust in personal judgment, or to a comfortable decision among confusing alternatives.

Making that tape, you'll have time to ground and center your concern for your child's health and happiness so you don't confuse it with your own. Otherwise your energies can confuse the kid and make life a lot more difficult! (It's a good idea to listen to the tape when you're finished to be sure the sound levels are good and that the narration is not confusing or unclear.)

Usually we work magic at Esbats, but some of our Sabbat rituals can *be* magical. This one was composed before we were formally Wiccan, but it still pleases us.

Rite of the Autumn Equinox
(1984)

Participants arrange themselves in a rough circle around an elf-light or group of candles. Each participant has matches. In unison, say:

> *We light these fires to our hopes for this season of harvest.*

Each puts a match to light the elf-light together, or in turn lights a candle. Each in turn shares a hope for the spiritual harvest. One says:

> *As tame and wild crops are the harvest of the Earth . . .*

All say:

> *So our visions and hopes are humanity's harvest.*

One says:

> *Nature directs us to gather in that which we have cultivated in ourselves . . .*

All say:

> *To reap what we have sown in the species' heart.*

One says:

As the harvest of the Earth begins . . .

All say:

> *Let us set at our table a place for our kin whose bodies hunger.*

One says:

> *Let us share as well the harvest of our hearts . . .*

All say:

> *And lay upon our altars that which we harvest of peace.*

One says:

> *We light these candles to the harvest of the human spirit . . .*

All say:

> *Where hope and fear become reality in the twilight of the cycle.*

One says:

> *We consecrate to this light, to the light of the visions within us, the work of our hands that manifests our hearts . . .*

All say:

> *That the work of our hands at harvest be the work of peace.*

One says:

> *The harvest of peace calls forth adobe (bricks) from hope . . .*

All say:

> *And peace is our shelter when Winter comes.*

In unison, say:

> *We light these candles to the hopes of our hearts for the harvest of our hands. We consecrate these candles to our hopes for this season of harvest. In the name of the planet, we conclude in peace.*

THE REDE AND THE LAW

In our magical work, we're guided by the Rede and the Three-fold Law. Introducing youngish children to magic, we must remember that their understanding of the ways we can harm others is different from ours. You must keep in mind that their interpretation of the Rede cannot be the same as ours.

It's very important not to wield the Rede and the Three-fold Law as clubs. It's easy to "guilt-trip" children (including those disguised as adults), and it hurts to be guilt-tripped. Adults often enough misinterpret the Law as an authoritarian rule that's enforced by a supernatural Big Brother. Children too young to think symbolically tend to take it quite literally, and taken like that, it becomes superstitious.

Instead of quoting the Law and the Rede to children in the primary grades, we can show them how to consider other people's feelings. "I wonder how it would feel to . . . ?" we can ask. "Has something like this ever happened to you?" "What do you think would feel good if _____ happened?"

These questions can't be asked accusingly, of course — and children's answers don't need to be coached or judged. If we want our kids to be able to work magic when they come of age, then we have to raise them with the magic of the Goddess' unconditional love, and trust that by our example and Hers, they will learn well.

It is not easy to live by Wiccan standards when our society presents us with so many obstacles to creative cooperation. But following Wiccan principles is actually a sort of spell, not spoken but expressed in our lifestyle, and a way to overcome those obstacles. The mundane ways you show your children will be every bit as important to them when they grow up as the rituals and chants you teach them.

If those mundane ways are consistent with the spiritual laws and rules of magic that we follow, then our lives and our children's will be closer to the God/dess, and the world will be a better place.

RITE OR WRONG?

We must have some concern, I think, about the materials we use. Canyondancer and I don't buy new leather or fur, but we do rescue it from the thrift shop now and again, mostly for ritual use. We buy very little at shops like the one where Faerie Moon and I find some material; and we do not contribute to the market of "exotics" at all.

When we do buy it, it is for ritual use, and is blessed to liberate the spirit of the animal from which it came. We never buy exotic leather or fur — cow and rabbit is our limit. No snake, no mink or jungle cat, and no exotic feathers, either. Except for an occasional little decorative bird at the craft shop, I don't buy feathers at all. If I need some, I can gather pigeon feathers almost anywhere. We find jay, woodpecker, "red birds" and sometimes hawk feathers when we camp.

If we want something more unusual than that, we go to the zoo and look beside the bird enclosures and beside the big animal habitats, where birds from the same region often live, too. I've had to be patient, but I've found everything from goose to guinea fowl feathers there, partridge to peacock.

When we camp, overnight or just for the day, I make it a point to look for bones, too. I've found quite a number of them, most of which now grace our backyard rockeries. Most of them come from cows, but from wild-ranging cows, not farm cows. We have some skulls, too, from squirrels and other small furries that we haven't identified.

We consider these finds — always treated reverently — to be gifts from the Gods. There is always energy left in them, energy we can feel. We respect this, and ask the spirit of the animal (even when we're not sure what it is!) to help make our yard and the Circle in it a safe and sacred place. We sometimes use these bones and feathers (and leather and fur) in charms or to decorate pouches. We've strung bird vertebrae on our Cords of Life at Mabon, for instance.

Although these pieces are more impressive than things with which we're more familiar — shells, for instance — it's good to remember that a lot of our materials were once alive. The paper this book is printed on used to be a tree.

The shells you may have on a necklace, in your fish bowl, or in a charm once protected a little water-creature. Cotton is harvested from living plants. Some plants are abused by modern farming techniques, as many animals are. The glass or ceramic mug from which you sip your tea was a mountain a million years ago, or maybe the sea bed.

Wicca teaches us that all of life is inter-related. Many of us reject the idea that humanity is the most important species on the planet, and hold that we have no right to extinguish any other forms on our own behalf. (Not as a species, anyway. One-on-one can be a little different.) We take this to mean that, when we decide what materials to use in mundane life or magical, we have to be satisfied that our use of it doesn't contribute to or result in its disappearing from the world.

Your family may make different decisions than we do about such materials. That's fine! The important thing is that you do *make a decision.* You should be able to explain to your children — and to anyone else who asks — why, in thealogical terms, if you will, you think it is or isn't okay to use certain materials in ritual or recreation.

Whether or not to hex or curse is another question that Wiccans face. It's one that every Witch and every family must answer, for the Three-fold Law knows no exceptions, and no one can take the responsibility of a curse for someone else.

Once when I was extremely angry, I asked the God to build a Gate in the offender's bones and "bring him face to face with the Guardians in his marrow." This is as close to hexing or cursing anyone as I have ever come — and as close as I ever will.

As you work, so are you worked. If you are willing to face the Guardian of the Gate, you are not out-of-bounds to challenge someone else to that experience. But honesty — naked in your rites, remember — is as important in magic as the incense and the flame.

"You can't heal if you can't hex" is a maxim we've all heard more than once. Does that mean that sometimes it's okay to curse somebody? We don't think so, and here's why.

Years ago, I was in the Explorer's room soothing him to sleep when — from my perspective — the room exploded. A rock had been hurled through the window by would-be burglars to see if anyone would be roused. Canyondancer checked on us first, so by the time he went outside, the hoodlums were gone, making plans after concluding that no one was home.

We took the Explorer into our bed and closed his door against wind through the broken window and so the cats wouldn't hurt their feet on the glass. Mindless vandalism, we thought, and didn't worry. We didn't sleep soundly, though, because the Explorer was very active in his sleep and it's hard to drift off with a foot in your ear! A couple of hours later, when the rock-throwers entered the house through the broken window, we were awake and heard them opening the door from the Explorer's room.

Canyondancer was on his feet immediately, thundering across the bed making fearsome noises. The intruders, at least as startled as we were, fled rather clumsily, knocking furniture about in their mad dash for the front door. They got nothing but a few bruises from the big wooden chair they ran into, and a good scare!

My experience was full adrenaline: I felt like a high-powered car in high gear with the pedal to the metal and the brakes on! I was shaking, and I was fierce, ready to defend my "cub." (I think the Explorer was about three-and-a-half years old then, and he slept through both the rock and the intrusion.)

I realized that if the burglars had followed their rock through the window, they would have been dead men, even though except for our wits and our body chemistry, we are an unarmed household. If either of us had gotten our hands on the intruders, they'd have been hospitalized at least, and we'd not have felt the tiniest bit of guilt. So what's the problem with hexing or cursing?

The problem is this: as individuals, our resources are limited. When we're suddenly confronted with danger (especially to our families), we may not be able to control the powerful hormonal responses that have evolved to keep human beings alive. Either one of us might have to kill an intruder with our bare hands to protect each other or our child.

But when we are doing magic, we are drawing on resources beyond the ordinary. When we do magic, we are between the Worlds, and the resources of all the Worlds are at our disposal. That means that there are more options open to us: creative, healing options that may not be available when we're facing an immediate physical danger.

Just as a city has more resources than a single household, a state has more resources than a city, and a nation has more resources than a state, so do Witches have greater resources in magical work than we or anyone else have in ordinary situations. We think that having all the Worlds' magic available to us obligates us to use it as consistently with Her laws as we can.

Nor do I demand aught of sacrifice, She tells us. *Love unto all beings is My law*. She is generous in giving us the powers of Her magic; shall we slap Her in the face with it?

MAGICAL CHILDREN

Mr. Rogers (yes, *that* Mr. Rogers), trying to help children cope with the tremendous guilt most of them accumulate, says that there's no such thing as magic, and that wishing can't make a thing happen. He's half-right. With very young children (and some adults, apparently) it's important to distinguish between wishes and magic, between "magical thinking" and magic; between fairy-tale magic and that which is real.

For children of any age, a wish can vent emotional energy the same way a romp in the playground vents physical energy; wishes can also express needs, and this is how we should understand them. The magic Witches do requires intellect and will that children do not possess. Adults' magic involves symbolic thinking and delaying gratification, capacities that small children do not have.

The fledgling magic children can do is the magic of belief and feeling; sometimes they can't tell the difference. Effortlessly, they see a castle where physically stands an unmade bed. Because they're not wearing the culture's yoke of agreed-upon reality, children can sincerely *act as if* almost anything!

Children need to become comfortable with Wiccan images early on so that the magic they do as initiated Wiccans will be its strongest. If the castle s/he built and played in as a little girl or boy is reconstructed as a temple or an astral retreat, its power will be amplified by that patina.

Children who grow up surrounded by Wiccan images and metaphors will find them in all their surroundings when they grow up. Their parents will have taught them where to look for Witchcraft, just as a lioness teaches her cubs where to look for nourishment. These children will not feel the discomfort of conversion their parents may have endured. For such a kid, full-fledged magic will come easily, because it will never have gone.

Properly directed, though, a child's energy can help to work real magic. It's usually not practical to bring a young child into a Circle to work magic with Mom and Dad, but his or her energy can be directed toward the magical goal at almost any other time.

"Let's pretend this doll is our friend Dawn, and let's sing a song to make her well again," works very nicely. "Let's put this *(unlit)* candle beside your bed so you can light up your dreams with it," might help kids with trouble sleeping. The Explorer has sent the energy he raises in his tae kwon-do class to a needy friend, releasing it toward its goal with every block and punch.

By incorporating elements of real magic into a child's activity, the child's energy is directed helpfully; the child will be familiar with the tools and techniques later on, when s/he joins Mom and Dad (or another coven) to work. (With young children, this integration should always be guided — a child shouldn't be given any techniques s/he's not free to work with in solitary play.)

Explaining magic to a child who lives in a culture that diminishes magic to special effects and stage tricks can be difficult. At about the same time that a child begins to grasp symbolic thinking, s/he is also developing the skills of logical reasoning, and the cultural influence can make a child skeptical.

The transition from childhood to adolescence produces great energy, energy which our culture teaches us to invest in insecurity and self-doubt in an effort to control the power it represents. Directing energy is Witchcraft's specialty, and a skill that once learned is ever-useful, especially when things get rough.

One way to introduce children to Wiccan ritual and magic is through their own magical logic. A favorite "blankie" spread out on the floor or the ground can be a child's first "Circle." (Fold under the edges of the blanket's corners if its square or rectangular shape bothers you; or fold them on top and let them mark the Quarters.) A favorite doll or stuffed toy can stand as a Goddess or God figure.

"Let's let Froofie be a wild animal and stand for the freedom of life in the forest," or "While Smiley Sally's on this blanket, she can be the Great Mommy of the whole world."

There's no reason your child's collection of dolls, figures or plush beasts can't make a Circle and work for Froofie's safe return from the washing machine, or for anything else that's important to your kid, either.

When the Explorer and his friends choose their "guys" from the toy box in the back room, they each mark out territories within which their "guys" (an eclectic group, I might add, from different sets and of different sizes and with different accessories, yet all quite cooperative with each other) are invulnerable. Before they get into the action, they mark their boundaries and make the rules for crossing them clear.

It's not far from this to defining the boundaries of a Circle and the rules for casting it, entering and leaving, and dismissing it. As you watch your kids play, you'll see lots of opportunities to say, "When you do this, it's kind of like when we . . ." or "When we do this, it's kind of like when you . . ." You may also be able to explain Wiccan practice to your kids' friends with such analogies, if and when that is appropriate.

Most of us experiment with skepticism, and as they get older, your kids probably will, too. It's an approach to logic, and it's okay. You don't have to worry if your kid wants her magic to stand to reason — because magic does. So much magic is obviously compatible with what we know of natural law that we can pretty easily trust that all of it is.

One way of making this clear to kids is in terms of examples from your own family life. "If you tell me that you want a chocolate cake for your birthday, you know that telling me is enough, right? You don't have to be there when I buy the mix or bake it to know it will be chocolate, do you? And you can trust that it's chocolate even if it has vanilla frosting, can't you?

"Just so, when we work magic, we're telling the Goddess what we need, and we know that's enough. We don't have to understand exactly how She works, and we don't have to worry if it looks different than we thought it would — has a different flavored frosting — either." You'll know what your kids wonder and worry about, and what metaphors and examples they'll understand. If you don't react defensively, if you accept their wary curiosity and work with it instead of against it, you'll be able to address their concerns effectively.

When your son or daughter says, "Aw, come on, how can that work?" don't be afraid to answer in material terms. Can't s/he tells when friends are angry or happy or scared, even if the friend says nothing or denies it? And doesn't a friend's mood affect you?

Have your children ever been worried about something, or totally immersed in sadness or fear, and then suddenly, when new information becomes available or somebody understands after all, been completely relieved?

Has a good friend ever done just the right thing, even when your kid didn't even know what s/he wanted that friend to do? Has something that interests your child ever, a day or so later, been all over the television and the papers and brought up by teachers and friends, out of the blue?

Right there, you have the basic mechanics of magic. It is possible — and your children will know this from their own experience as soon as you point it out to them — to influence and be influenced by other people and the world *by and through energy.*

Wicca is a religion of experience, and you can show your children how to interpret their experience in Wiccan terms (as well as in scientific and psychological terms). And that little "oh" that you hear from them or see in their eyes or smiles of understanding? That's magic, too.

Some Simple Rituals and Magics

The spiral is an ancient symbol of the process of life, and holds great power. It is an image that speaks volumes and transcends cultural distinctions. When you use it in a spell, you call upon tens of thousands of years of human energy and add it to your own. Here are some spiral spells that you and your children can use in your work.

The Salt Spiral

You will need a plain white sheet of paper (or a white paper napkin or an undecorated paper plate), a crayon in a color suitable to your purpose, and salt.

Salt is a symbol of the Earth's strength and purity. Before you cast this spell, bless the salt. Draw a pentagram over it (right in the box is fine) and say:

> *Blesséd be, you creature of Earth. Banish all fear from this place and bless my work with your strength.*

With the crayon, draw a dot or symbol in the center of the paper. This represents the work you want to do, your goal. Focus your mind on this goal. Starting at the outer edge of the paper, draw an in-winding spiral with the salt, finishing with a small mound to cover the dot in the center. Think or talk about your goal as you draw the spiral.

When you have put your energy into the spiral of salt, press both your thumbs into the mound of salt to seal your work. Sealing the spell this way binds your energy to the spell and allows it to keep receiving energy from the world. After you have sealed the spell, fold the paper so that all the salt comes to the center.

If you spill any, moisten your finger and put the salt on your tongue to make the spell a part of you. Now, either bury the folded paper in your yard, or put it in a pouch and hang it somewhere safe. Every time you walk near it or see it, you'll recharge it and keep it working. When the goal has been achieved, you may burn the paper with some words of thanks.

The Yarn Spiral

For this work you'll need a large open space (a big, grassy yard or park would be great) and a skein of yarn in a color suitable for your purpose. Let your child choose the color, for children make very strong associations, and insisting on an orthodox correspondence may divert their energy. Choose a word or a short phrase to represent your goal.

Your child should hold the pulling end of the yarn (the one from the inside, not the outer one) to her solar plexus, where the ribs meet just below the middle of the chest. You'll need to hold the skein of yarn and make sure it doesn't get hung up and interrupt the working. (You can let small knots or tangles go by; just keep the yarn feeding until the spell is done.)

Your child should begin turning in a circle, slowly at first, and chanting the word or phrase that represents the goal. Gradually, your child will spin faster and faster, getting wrapped in the yarn, and probably dizzy. S/he may stagger or even fall down. If that happens, shout the word or phrase as the child falls. If the child doesn't fall, s/he should keep going till the yarn is gone, and then fall down on purpose, shouting the word or phrase.

The Explorer charges appropriately-colored yarn with the energy of his spinning dance, working a simple spell that children of any age can do to achieve a specific goal.

Without unwinding the yarn (make nine knots and break the strand between the last knot and the skein if there's any left), slide this enormous spiral off your child. This spiral has been wound toward the outside, sending its energy toward the goal. The yarn can be kept as a charm, knotted to intensify the spell, or burned (outside, please — it won't smell pleasant, and you might like to burn some incense at the same time) to seal it forever and send additional energy through fire and air.

Story Spells

Children love to tell stories. You can help your child cast a story spell with — yes, construction paper! — and scissors. Cut out shapes to represent the characters in the story, which are the elements of the spell. If, for instance, you want to help someone get well, you might cut out the shape of a bed, the patient, and another figure to represent your child. Let your child choose the color(s) of paper, and if s/he's old enough, design and cut the figures, too.

Using the cut out figures, enact the healing. Let your child act it out, dancing the figures around on the table and telling a story of recovery. If you child is working on a self-healing, the third cut-out might represent the Goddess, or the God, or another comforting figure.

When the story has been told (maybe several times), your child can make a symbol on each figure — initials or a healing symbol — and put all the figures in an envelope with the patient's figure on top of the others. Then your child can mail the envelope to the patient, or put it under their pillow. When the situation is resolved, your child can, if s/he's old enough or with your supervision, burn the envelope with some words of thanks.

This is a form of sympathetic magic. Our ancestors left their figures on the cave walls. If your child would prefer to draw the story spell, great! Older children may want to write the stories and even read them to the person they're meant to help, or to someone who can influence the outcome of the situation s/he's working on.

I did some story magic when I was young, before I knew what it was. I wrote about marrying a professor and having a son, which is exactly what I did when I grew up. And when a high-school friend and I wrote completely fantastic stories that combined elements of the First World War with our concerns about Viet Nam, we were astonished to find elements of those stories appearing in the paper!

One of our characters was the Red Baron, who reappeared in Viet Nam with a pet boa constrictor, of all things. About a week after we wrote that, there was a photo in the (Portland) *Oregonian* of a young medic whose nickname was the Red Baron, and who had a pet boa! I can, therefore, recommend story spells with great confidence.

No magic can contravene natural law, but natural law works through energy, and we can influence energy. When energy is in motion, when "things are happening," we sometimes want to give that energy a nudge in one direction or another. Story spells are one kind of nudge; this candle magic is another.

Tipping the Scales

You will need two candles, one to represent the way things seem to be going, and one to represent the way you'd like them to go. Make these two candles as different in color as you can. It is up to you whether to use votives, tapers, pillars, or more decorative candles; some shops carry candles in a variety of shapes, maybe you can find one that will pretty much exactly represent the work you mean to do.

Set up the "seems to be" candle and light it while you think about the situation you'd like to influence. As you watch the flame, think or talk about the way you'd like to change what seems to be happening. When you have a clear picture of the change you'd like to effect, pick up the "like to be" candle and hold it in both hands.

Concentrate for a few moments on the change you'd like to see. Then, when that image is very strong, light the "like to be" candle from the "seems to be" candle, and *immediately* extinguish the "seems to be" candle with your moistened thumb and forefinger. (Obviously, this spell is not appropriate for very young children to work. If your kid is old enough to light candles like this, but not eager to put one out this way, s/he can spit into a snuffer and use that. The point is to put some of yourself into extinguishing the "seems to be" candle.)

If possible, let the "like to be" candle burn down. If you can't do that, then let it burn for as many minutes as your child is years old, and extinguish it the same way you did the "seems to be" candle. Then burn the "like to be" candle that many minutes every day until it has burned away, even if things work out the way you want before the candle's gone.

Young children can stomp their feet rhythmically and chant to raise energy. They can release that energy toward a goal by jumping onto a picture they've drawn of the goal. They can draw pictures in dirt or sand and dance the Witches' Rune; you can chant and drum while your child dances.

With their fingers they can stir a bowl of salt, making signs that represent what they want to happen, and then fling the charged salt into the air. All eyes should be closed when the salt is flung; partly to symbolize trust that the Mother will use the energy in the service of life, and partly to protect your eyes from the flying salt, which can burn painfully.

You will think of other ways to use traditional Wiccan symbols and tools (and to modify the spells in this book and in others, adapting them to your kids' ages and needs) to introduce your children to magic, and your children will have some ideas, too.

There are, of course, two parts to working any magic: the *magic* and the *working*. A child's work is different from an adult's, but just as important. What we all need to remember is that magic is alive through us, through our lives, and the more energy we put into our magic and into our lives, the better both our lives and our magic will be.

5

ANSWERING THE HARD QUESTIONS

Every parent, and most friends, eventually has to answer hard questions for children and other people. Why did someone I love do such a terrible thing? Why did such a terrible thing happen to someone I love? Why am I alive? What's all this stuff about sex, anyway? Why do people think we're Satanists? Was that my fault? What happens when I die?

We think it's terribly important to answer these questions in Wiccan terms. Sometimes we have to rephrase the question before we can answer it. You can't answer a question like *Why does one plus one equal three?* because one plus one *doesn't* equal three; you can't answer a question like *Why does God want me to suffer?* either. Here are some of our questions and answers — and remember, questions that have been asked for thousands of years take more than 30 seconds to answer!

Why am I alive? Well, Mommy and Daddy love each other very much, and when a man and woman love each other very much . . . If that's not the answer the kid's looking for, try this: because Life is the nature of the universe.

There are questions to which the answer really is "because that's the way it is." Stephen Hawking in *A Brief History of Time* says that questions about what was before the Big Bang are not only impossible to answer but irrelevant, because the Bang was a *singularity:* something that, when it happens, changes things so much that afterwards is utterly, indescribably, incomparably different than anything that was before.

So it is, we think, with Life. Once the Goddess saw Herself in the mirror, once Her joy exploded, nothing was the same. The Big Bang was material, the Goddess' creation of consciousness its spiritual aspect. And it is the nature of each that they are metaphors for the other.

They are inseparable and yet distinguishable, and inevitable. We are alive because we evolved because there were atoms from which we could evolve because there was a Bang because the Goddess is and existence is Her nature.

Okay, but what are we supposed to do about it? Ah, well, that one's a little easier. We're supposed to do as we will, an we harm none. We're supposed to love all beings. We're supposed to be aware (of our needs, for instance, so that whenever we have any, we can gather in some sacred place).

Other religions assert that humanity's purpose is to serve and glorify a god. Generally they are quite specific about which god and how to serve and glorify. The Goddess calls all acts of love and pleasure Her rituals, so that the solitary enjoyment of a summer's afternoon is as worshipful as a formal Circle, but worship is only one way Wiccans fulfill Life's purpose.

Being a religion of experience rather than dogma, Wicca holds that the purpose of Life is — Life. So when the Explorer wants to know why he's alive, we tell him that he's alive to experience as much as he can. To love, to create, to run in the wind, to cry, to hope, to dream. To chill his toes in mountain streams, to watch the ants on the sidewalk, to ask how to spell p-l-a-t-y-p-u-s, to drift into oneness with the atmosphere half-way up the mountain. To see in the darkness of a cave, to hold another hand in a Circle under the Moon, to keep his Maypole ribbon tight as we dance, to pet the cat.

And when he wants to know *is that all?* we ask him what else he imagines there might be, and you know what? He smiles in that sudden secret understanding that is, ultimately, the only reason any of us need for Life.

Why do bad things happen? Am I bad? No! "Bad" things happen for a number of reasons. Sometimes they are the natural consequences of hasty, uninformed, or misinformed choices. Sometimes they're the result of some else's ignorance, fear, or chemical incompleteness. Sometimes they are beyond human control. A distinction we use is between *something we did wrong* and *something that happened to us.*

We don't talk about fault or blame — we talk about responsibility. Fault and blame imply guilt, and guilt keeps us powerless; responsibility implies authority and the power to correct and learn from our mistakes. That power is the Goddess' gift to all of us; we don't presume to deny it.

Sometimes a thing that seems bad when it happens turns out to be the proverbial blessing in disguise. The Goddess, as we all know, works in mysterious ways. More practically than that, though, some of the things we call bad could be called something else: an inconvenience, a Challenge, an opportunity, a change in plans.

Although it can be difficult to find purpose and inspiration in everything that happens, it is a worthwhile undertaking. When things proceed according to plan it's easy to take things for granted. When our expectations are challenged by random occurrences — a burglar's strike, an inexplicable stroke — you may be laid low.

While you are thus sprawled upon the ground, you have an opportunity to explore its depths and strengths — and your own depths and strengths as well. You don't have to just bite the dust or eat dirt: you can choose to be nourished.

Changing your perception of something that's happened sometimes gets you laughed at, but it is the heart of magic. Another way of appreciating the value of changed perspective is sociopolitical: are men who have long hair and beards, for example, dang-blasted sissy commie-pinko bums — or are they fully masculine, free and natural?

At the Explorer's tae kwon-do class, I overheard a conversation between two dads that illustrates this point wonderfully. Putting his pocket Bible down for a moment, one asked the other if he'd let his son grow long hair. The second father answered that he might, as long as it wasn't too long.

"To his shoulders?" the first dad asked.

"Oh, no!" the second exclaimed. "I think boys should look like boys."

Sitting next to them, it was all I could do not to say that my favorite picture of their Jesus has always been the one with his hair in a crew cut.

Is it a curse that Canyondancer was unable to find a job teaching political science at a liberal arts university, or the gateway to his destiny?

If you'd asked us that when we first found out that his position at a small school in Missouri wasn't tenure-track after all, when we had a mountain of debts and the Explorer was barely a year old, when we had to wire my parents for money to pay the movers who'd upped their price at the last minute, we might have called it a bad thing.

But now we call it the first step on the path to the lives we live now, and we wouldn't trade them for all the honest movers in Missouri or all the tenured contracts in Academia.

Is there no divine punishment for evil-doing? No, we do not believe there is — only the healing, only the learning, only the wholeness. *But it seems so unfair!* Does it? Love unto all beings is Her law. Punishment is revenge, revenge is fear, and fear precludes love. One of my favorite chants is *Where there's fear there can be no love/Where there's love there can be no fear.*

Self-realization is love, and in the Summerland, we realize our selves and our Self. And on Earth, the natural consequences of unloving behavior are severe — the solitary confinement to which we are sentenced by so many social norms is punishment enough.

This does not mean that unacceptable behavior has to be tolerated, it only means that we will protect ourselves from it most effectively if we act from love rather than succumbing to the same fear that motivates a wrong-doer, if we draw upon the resources cooperation gives us rather than accepting the isolation wrong-doers feel.

Why did someone I love do such a bad thing? Fear, most likely. Of course, there are people whose brains are chemically incomplete: "glitchy," we call it, but fear can be just as crippling as an organic chemical imbalance. Whether a bad thing is done "by choice" or without control, there is fear behind it. Ironically, the most heinous offenses are usually committed out of the fear of being unloved.

And how should we respond to the people who do these bad things? First, we must restrain them. We must do so from an understanding of their pain; yes, their pain. Love unto all beings cannot manifest if we don't acknowledge others' needs as equally important to our own. Then we must provide for them an environment in which their fear is diminished. Otherwise, we only nurture the perversion of nature that moved them to act wrongly.

Above all, we must not give in to our own fear. Whether we're talking about violence on the streets or our children's smart-mouthing, loss of control is scary. Our ancestors lived in peace for tens of thousands of years in an environment over which they had much less control than we exercise today; how is it that our society is so impotent?

We think it has a lot to do with unrealistic expectations. Witches do not appreciate the fundamentalist expectation, for instance, that everyone on the planet should accept Jesus as their personal savior. But white America cannot seem to understand that other cultures might not appreciate an expectation that they will adopt WASP standards of beauty, of social structure, of personal worth.

If we shared the Goddess' unconditional love with each other — Her sheer joy and Her courage, Her daring, Her humor, Her sense of adventure — we could appreciate our differences, and not hide from them or deny them or condemn them. With our fear of each other gone, we would not need to interact defensively.

I sometimes talk about fields of wildflowers, pointing out the cultural consensus that variety in that context is good. Then I wonder aloud why, when we can appreciate the natural variety of hundreds of kinds of flowers, we get so uptight about the natural variety of the rest of life, including ourselves.

The transformation of a society as rewarding of aggression as ours is, of institutions as bureaucratically defended as ours are, is not something that can be achieved overnight. But it is something that can be achieved, if we do not cloud our vision with fear.

The transformation of a bully into a friend is not easy, but it is, as boomers are wont to say, "do-able." The force that is life in all its complexity is not incapable of such a thing, and we are that force, for that is God/dess.

What about this sex business, anyway? The only time sex is bad is when it is a business. Anything people do together is bad when it's exploitive. There's nothing intrinsically bad about sex, though, and nobody's body isn't beautiful.

Overhearing preadolescent conversations, it's painfully clear that a lot of children know nothing about the urges they're beginning to feel. They know some "dirty words" but they're abysmally ignorant of their own anatomies and what changes to expect — somebody's got hair, the others will exclaim, so — so he has to use deodorant.

The presumption that nothing about our bodies is good, or at least not good enough, comes partly from religious teachings that the physical world belongs to the devil and partly from the modern culture's narrow definitions of beauty and success, and the sense of unworthiness is all-pervasive. Our bodies are "nasty," as the kids put it; our children may leave that notion behind, but many of their friends never will.

From their ignorance and a premise that bodies are fundamentally bad, how can they appreciate any experience their bodies give them? Instructed that their bodies belong to the devil and are displeasing to their god — an instruction reinforced by beatings and mockery that are taken for granted in more families than you'd like to think — how can they respect anyone else's body?

How will they trust their instincts if their instincts are vilified and repressed? How will they value their lives? The sad truth is that many of them won't — and the sadder truth is that when they grow up, they'll be part of a whole society that does not love its body, politic or physical. This horrific attitude contributes to the problems of drug addiction, crime, homelessness, and other cultural corruption.

Much of the fear most people feel, physically, socially, economically, comes from their understanding of their bodies — and by extension, the rest of their selves — as bad, unworthy. The conflict that patriarchal monotheism has deliberately constructed between our hormones and our higher selves is not natural; accepting it as such makes us schizophrenic.

We believe that the Goddess gave us both sides of our brains and the connecting organ so we can live in wholeness. Patriarchal faiths have cut the connection, much as mental patients used to be lobotomized so they'd be easier to control.

They say that with the AIDS epidemic, the sexual revolution is over. We say it has not yet begun; what looked like revolution at first turned out to be just getting dizzy. Promiscuity is not freedom, it's just slavery to a different master; the Goddess both blesses us and charges us with freedom from slavery. Notches on the shaft aren't the signature of joy; mindlessness is neither love nor pleasure.

The fear that still guides our society's sexual quest only makes us aggressive: fear makes us defensive, and we're told that the best defense is a good offense. There is no such thing as a good offense, though; and neither an erect penis nor an open vulva is offensive. Rather, they are sacred, they are Life itself. That's what about all this sex business.

The joy can be restored, of this we are sure. If passionate rhetoric is not your family's style, there are other ways of communicating healthy sexual attitudes. If your focus is on respect for privacy, which goes beyond the toilet and the toilette, rather than on concealment of body parts, then skyclad needn't ever feel naughty. If you use "real names" for your anatomies — *penis,* not "wee-wee," and *vagina,* not "down there" — then more subtle non-clinical metaphors will not be meaningless or uncomfortable.

We have to remember that before we come through puberty, we don't appreciate sex. We can understand it intellectually once we're seven or so, and even more technically, but until we're pubescent, we don't get behind it emotionally. Our kids are going to roll their eyes and wrinkle their noses and go, *Eeeewww, girls!* or *Eeeewww, boys!* It doesn't mean they'll never have a merry May Day!

Most parents have been interrupted at love-making by their children. The popular culture laughs at this situation, making rather crude jokes to mask discomfort. The awkwardness and fear that witnessing the sex act will warp our kids comes from guilt, imposed by patriarchal custom. All acts of love and pleasure are the Goddess' rituals, though.

When the three of us hug all together, as we often do, we call it a "together hug." When the Explorer was very young and came into our room one night while we were at love, we paused to see what he would say or do. He approached us with a sleepy smile and outstretched arms, and said: "Can I have some of that together hug?"

Of course he could! We each reached out an arm, the three of us embraced; he went back to bed, and we went back to our midnight motion. I think the same thing happened a few more times while he was still small, and the Explorer shows no sign of being warped. What he does show signs of is trusting, and knowing that love can be everywhere.

Whether he was ever aware that we were having sex, I do not know. He is aware that people do; he knows "where babies come from" because he's seen the pictures of his own birth, and he's attended two other home births.

He also understands that sex is only part of love, and only one of the body's many wonderful capacities. Unlike some of his friends (and some of ours, and some of yours, too, no doubt) he understands that not all hugs and smiles between men and women are sexual. In other words, because he has not been taught that anything about his body is taboo, nothing is.

Oh, he knows that we all need privacy, most of us for things like going to the bathroom (although with only one bathroom in the house, some sharing is necessary). He knows that there are some pleasures of the body that we don't share with other people, or only with very special other people. But that's not because our bodies or our selves are unworthy.

It's because some pleasures and parts of our bodies and souls are so special that we want to share them only with people who are equally special, and special in certain ways. One picks one's companions on the Quest very carefully, after all, not on the spur of the moment on the basis of one or two tastes in common.

We need to respect our children's feelings so they can respect their feelings, and feel comfortable with them all their lives. Otherwise, we risk teaching our children to acknowledge only certain feelings, skewing their perception and disabling them emotionally.

Sex is a matter of life and death in more ways than one; that's why it's sacred to us. And that's why it's important —

a moral obligation, really — to address it as families. Like death, sex is an agent of transformation, a holy mystery.

Our culture tries to take initiation into that mystery for granted. We've become conditioned to instant gratification. From television, for instance, we learn that problems should be solved in half an hour, or an hour at most, and that a lot of the work to solve them is done invisibly, during the commercials. (This is an example of "magical" or "fairy-tale thinking.")

Consequently, the significance of sex and other important aspects of our lives has been distorted, its real meaning hidden in obsession and subjugated to commercialism. We've been robbed of our natural joy, forced to be defensive and insensitive. On top of that, we're overwhelmed by the violence of unresolved anger and grief for our loss.

As Wiccans, we believe it is within our power to restore the natural balances. But we must also be willing to undertake the initiatory task of both-brain awareness to restore the sanctity of our sexuality.

Why do some people think we're Satanists? Because a long time ago, when the Christian armies were expanding their empires, they found native pagan populations uncooperative. Just as invaders do now, they called the natives sub-human. Misinterpreting indigenous customs they did not understand, the conquerors tried to make sense of unfamiliar religions by standards that did not legitimately apply. The sense they made was that it was all right to slaughter these people, all right to burn their temples and enslave their children.

And all right to excoriate their faith and demean their gods — our Goddess and God! — even all right to invent new interpretations of their own faith so that our conquered ancestors' gods could be more easily vilified.

Too hard to explain? Try an analogy of playground or office politics. Call the "enemy" names, deliberately misinterpret questions and conversations, even lie. Arrange mistakes that will seem to be the "enemy's" fault. Recruit allies with empty promises. It's a dire story, old and new at the same time.

What historical details our children and the rest of our families are ready to hear is different for each of us, but the situation can be made plain to anyone of any age. It's not Christian-bashing to tell this truth; we did not ask to be enslaved and burned, nor did the Christians we know today forge the chains or light the fires. Nor, for that matter, was it always Christians who attacked our ancestral cultures.

There are still some people who walk around with Bics and kindling in their pockets. Their credibility is diminishing because they have told (or maybe just believed) so many lies about us that their stories are not straight. Our story is long, but consistent, and the more we tell it, the more trusted it — and we — will be.

DEATH

Death is one of popular culture's last taboos. No one wants to face it except in contexts so protected that we are not really touched. Sad or gory movies let us project our fear and guilt; even when death is almost dripping into our laps from the big and little screens, we don't have to face it.

In real life, death is more than a special effect, and as our society thrashes about in waste, destruction, hypocracy, cynicism and hopelessness, we more and more often have to face it. Because death and loss are a part of everyone's life, and because we are so detached by social customs, we think it's very important for Wiccan families to be aware of Witchcraft's perspectives. Otherwise, we'll be unprepared and afraid — untrusting and loveless — when we get to the Gates, and that's a fate truly worse than death.

When the young son of a man I know was very seriously injured in an accident, I was called to the hospital to minister to the parent. He is not a Wiccan, but his own minister was out of town, and his estranged family lived in distant states. He knew a little about Witchcraft from some of our conversations, and his secret hope was that I could wave my magic wand and change medical reality, which was grim.

What I could do for him, and what proved to offer more comfort than the fear and guilt that were the foundations of his early religious training, was hold him and let him cry, and help him face the very real possibility of his not-yet-ten-year-old son's death. Church members rallied around in the waiting room, but no one was comfortable with his tears, and no one would say "the D-word."

Sometimes there is no sense to be made of things. This is difficult to accept, and especially in the absence of a strong conviction that the world is by nature "friendly," the temptation to lay blame is strong. But he was not a bad parent to have a son who was walking one day in the wrong place at the wrong time; no god was punishing the boy for breaking his father's rules. No one was at fault; it was a horrible accident.

Serious accidents, like chemical imbalances in our brains, or birth defects, are glitches in the natural order, not demonstrations of the fundamental hostility of life. They do not happen for the reasons we misunderstand karma to provide. We give them reason, we choose to let these events change our lives, and we make the deaths we mourn meaningful, not in vain.

These accidents do not happen deliberately to punish us because we have in our sinfulness thrown life out of balance. Rather, when these accidents divert life's creativity, it is within our natural power to restore the balance by our response to physical, emotional, and social trauma.

This restoration of senseless death or loss to the service of life cannot be accomplished from feelings of fear or guilt, but the restoration we make of it becomes, through our own power and by our own choice, the reason for the loss. The loss hasn't any inherent reason, but *we* do.

And our restorative energy is generated by love and trust, the same love and trust in which Wiccans re/enter the Circle. Grief need not ever be denied, but fear and guilt need not always attend it. When dogmatically imposed fear and guilt do attend grief, it cannot regenerate or heal as it is biochemically and spiritually meant to do.

Nor do I demand aught of sacrifice, for behold, I am the Mother of all things, and My love is poured forth across the Lands.

A death in the family can feel like a sacrifice, but the Goddess is true to her word. Death is not a sacrifice, for you need give up nothing to it: life's forms change, but Life does not end.

A life's influence is not diminished by its transformation, either. Knowing that the spirit is eternal, you can trust that love — a function of spirit — is eternal, too.

Indeed, beyond death, freed from the limitations of a physical body, love's expressions can be even greater.

On Earth, I give knowledge of the Spirit Eternal, and beyond death, I give peace, and freedom, and reunion with those who have gone before.

Though "letting go" of a dying loved one or accepting other drastic changes is painful, you know you are not turning your belovéd or yourself out into some trackless wilderness. No, you are releasing that spirit to the care of our Mother — Who better to care for those you love? Through the Mother we are all reborn — the very life you are living right now is beyond death.

What happens when I die? People who have returned from death tell us that they leave their bodies to survey the scene. Despite the surprise they may feel, they are usually calm, and can often remember conversations held over their bodies.

Then they are distracted and drawn into a long tunnel, which is sometimes noisy and alarming, but which always becomes a light that is more than a light, a sort of living incandescence.

Virginia Woolfe associated incandescence with genius, suggesting that genius cannot find expression through a mind that has not burned away all bitterness, fear, and other such distractions. The Goddess promises freedom beyond death; freedom from those very impediments to our natural genius for life. She is, after all, that which is attained at the end of all desire, "desire" meaning the basic mortal needs and senses by which you are aware of being separate from the Whole.

As people die, sometimes the living light alone greets them; sometimes they perceive it as a welcoming figure. There is never any fear once a person has seen the light.

Wicca calls the experience of this serene light the *Summerland.* We have told our son about the tunnel, and we explained to him that the light's embrace is a "together-hug with the Goddess and the God." Thus death is a healing, a loving restoration rather than a punishing destruction. Any hurts and confusions there might have been in the body or in the mind are transformed.

We are challenged by death to see beyond the material plane, to resensitize our perception to other dimensions. Talk of worlds "beyond the veil" is not placebic platitude. There are other Worlds. They are accessible in many other cultures, and can be accessible in ours.

You can't see the wind, but you can feel its presence. You can't see loved ones whose bodies you have laid to rest, but you can feel their presence if you let yourself. You notice the wind's workings when you admire a sailing kite or find shapes in the clouds. You can notice the ways in which your loved ones affect the world, too, if you allow yourself to have that vision.

But it is possible to bundle up so securely against the weather that you can't feel the wind. And it is possible to be so guilt-ridden and afraid of death that you cannot perceive it as a part of life, too.

What the Goddess requires of you is not sacrifice, but trust, and you have already committed yourselves to that trust in your dedications and initiations. Her love is poured forth across the Lands — the spirit that animates your loved ones will be reborn, and through love and trust that we will merry meet again in Her reunion.

These are complex feelings, and our perception of them has been distorted by an adversarial, authoritarian, patriarchal culture. Wiccans of various traditions and experience need to come to a fearless, guiltless understanding of the relationship of death to life, each in their own ways.

Culturally, death is still taboo. But if all acts of love are Her rituals, and love unto all beings is Her law, then we have a moral obligation to the God/dess, to ourselves, and to our children to face the Guardian at that Gate.

In practical terms, it's a good idea to sort these things out before anyone is in mortal peril. If your family is part of a coven, suggest to your HPs an exploration of cultural and Wiccan attitudes toward death.

A Circle to talk about your own death is interesting. Write your own epitaph, select your own music, imagine the site where you'd like your remains to rest. If your family Circles alone, find times and places to talk about death. Mortality, remember, is not morbid, it is sacred, and is blasphemed by guilt and fear.

Should children take part in such exercises? Probably. You don't have to present the subject as harshly as the culture does. "What music do you think would be nice to play when you go to greet the Gods?" you can ask. "When you move away from this World, what would you like your friends to remember about you?" If you think about it, you'll be able to ask questions like these that won't scare your children, and that will give them some sense of control over their lives and deaths.

When families talk about these things together, children learn other things, too. They learn, for instance, not to discount what you're saying just because you're crying when you say it. They learn that death is natural, sad but not bad. They learn that it's a good idea to take a look at your life now and then to remind yourself to live it the way you want.

If you've talked about it before somebody dies, then none of you have to face your loss and the unknown at the same time. Also, you won't be as vulnerable to the Victorian inclination to pull away from each other in a crisis if you've practiced coming together.

If someone you love is dying, maybe you can give that person an opportunity to share some feelings, to ask some questions, to express some preferences. You'll cry, I guarantee it, but tears are cleansing — have a good cry, you'll feel better! And when you come right down to it, wouldn't you rather be with people who won't hide from the important feelings, instead of finding yourself emotionally alone at the end of your life, or a part of it?

You're supposed to have to summon up your courage to face death. Death is that transition for which all others are preparatory. Death's path to rebirth is the adventure for which all mythical and legendary Quests are metaphors. Can we bear it? Certainly we can, because the Goddess is with us, from the beginning and at the end of all desire.

Following — metaphorically — Starhawk's advice to follow the self to find the Self, we find that approaching our lives with reverence (and mirth) really does transform the mundane into the spiritual. Treating our ordinary lives with the same respect we give to our religious activities is one way to teach kids the sensitivity to perspective — attitude — that is so important in both realms.

6

MOONS AND SUNS

One of the things our family likes to do is camp. (Canyon-dancer was named for his skill in dancing a Volkswagen bus through southern Arizona's canyons.) There are some beautiful places here in southeastern Arizona. What they call "sky islands," pine and oak forest oases, rise 5-9,000 feet from the desert floor, and they're perfect for celebrating Sabbats!

Every January, we sit down with the calendar and choose the vacation days I'll take from work. Instead of taking my whole two weeks at once, we take a day here and two or three days there so we can camp a three- or four-day weekend more than once between Eostara and Samhain. We're experimenting with setting our Esbats for the year in January, too, so we can arrange to be where we want on the Full Moons, and so that all of us can be free on the same night.

If you can, try arranging your vacation schedule around the Sabbats and your family's favorite activities. It feels really good to reintegrate reverence, finding the sacred in the mundane. All acts of pleasure are Her rituals, and we honor Her with mirth as well as with reverence. Think about this the next time you have some time off, and see what a nice guided tour the Goddess gives!

Decorated with sprays of the Tombstone rose that arches over the circle, Campsight's bright altar is set up for Brigid and the Coven's dedication, the brand-new Coven banner hanging near the ramada.

MOONS

Our backyard is small. When we bought our apartment-sized row house, the back was hard dirt and the landscaping was construction debris. Now, after 15 years, a circle of grass in an adobe patio is surrounded by woodsy rockeries that have come home with us from camping trips.

Fallen branches, some of them livewood, decorate the cyclone fence. A cascading Tombstone rose arches up over the East, blooming like sunrise every Spring. In the buffer zone between the Circle and the carport, there are garden boxes, two of them. In one, our old Siamese cat and a pet rat are buried, and wild catnip sprawls across the crystals that mark the graves.

Because our blood families have lived in Oregon for several generations and the family cemeteries are there, the animals' graves in our yard stand for all the burial places of our people. When we want, we can sit by these graves and commune with generations of ancestors, all the way back to Britain and Normandy, all the way back to the Caves. If you've buried pets in the backyard, so can you!

Adobe-brick altars stand at the North and South on our wild-growing grass Circle. Near the South there's a redwood ramada, soon to hold a terra-cotta Mexican fireplace. In the meantime, we make do with the Weber bonfire. This is our Covenstead, and it is here in this Circle that we usually observe the Moons.

One summer, the three of us were at Sunset Crater (between Flagstaff and the Grand Canyon, in northern Arizona) at a Full Moon. A few miles from our site in the National Monument's campground, we found a clearing to cast our Circle.

Lava gravel rolled beneath our feet, 15-foot lava cliffs jutted starkly up against a clear sky, and in the moonlight, lithe silver-white aspen, leaves dancing, shimmered. Our music and voices were the only other sounds — even the night birds were quiet.

We were so moved and inspired by that experience that since then we've taken a couple of opportunities to circle in the desert that surrounds Tucson. Faerie Moon and the Norseman live a few miles past the city lights, so sometimes we hike a few minutes from their front yard and cast our Circle on a low desert hill. When we do, there are six of us, for their beautiful husky, Banshee, comes along!

At our Moons, we do magic. Sometimes we do candle magic, burning a small beeswax candle and chanting until it's gone, or letting the descending flame release a needle or a disc. Sometimes we concentrate on a common image. Usually we chant or sing; our chants are sometimes traditional, and sometimes not. *All we are saying is give (peace, love, health, Earth, life) a chance . . .* is one we like to use, too.

We work for ourselves and each other, and for our friends, and for the world. Sometimes we charge talismans to protect a long-term goal. Sometimes we work for love, sometimes for health, sometimes for success. Faerie Moon often brings her special poppy-seed bread, and I think our magic works better when she's baked it!

We wear black robes without hoods to Esbats, and we are barefoot when reasonable caution allows. (Stepping on scorpions is not required, but we don't let gravel or a few stickers daunt us.) The Explorer wears his pentacle, Canyon-dancer sometimes a gold ankh, and I wear special crystals or other stones, to charge them or to call upon their power.

Sometimes we do other Moons, usually New, with other Witches, often in secluded areas of public parks. Using the Witches' Rune, we'll dance on drawings we've made in the sand, or we'll raise sound energy and direct it in a healing. At these street-clothed, candle-less gatherings, we can practice new Quarter calls or invocations and new ways of working, and we usually share a pot-luck feast when the work is done.

You might need to do something less obvious. A picnic dinner in the park and a conversation about the beginnings you'd like to work on can be a proper New Moon — it's up to you! Children's energy is naturally suited to New Moon work, of course, for children are just beginning, too.

SUNS

We meet for Sabbats (sometimes we call them Suns) and Esbats with Faerie Moon and the Norseman. We call ourselves the Campsight Coven because we've been camping together at least as long as we've been Witches together. Every year we try to observe at least one Sabbat in the woods. (We plan for more, but plans have to be flexible, and yours are probably flexed as often as ours are!)

It seems to us that the rules for successful camping — plan ahead, be ready for rain, leave it cleaner than you found it, and so on — are pretty good rules for living anywhere. In town, between the Worlds, anywhere. We named our coven after this way of seeing things, our *camp sight.*

For the last several years we've celebrated Beltane with a camping trip to a different site each year. I'm willing to hold most Sabbats on the closest weekend, but I prefer to start celebrating Beltane on May first. In 1991 CE,

IN HONOR

OF

_____

_____

THIS DONATION IS MADE

BY

_____

Food Bank Donation Card

when it fell on a Wednesday, that preference required a five-day weekend!

Dancing a Maypole with only five people is hard — you really need an even number. So after a couple of years, we started inviting other Wiccans to share our Beltane.

Now several Witches from the Tucson Area Wiccan Network (TAWN) make the roughly two-and-a-half hour trek to the mountains for the long weekend. Believe me, a Maypole dances much better with sixteen than with five! Many another camper, and a ranger or two, has seen or heard our revels, and you know what? No one's ever bothered us! Not even the officers at the inspection station on the Arizona/New Mexico border have questioned the Maypole lashed to our luggage rack.

But Beltane's not the only Sabbat, and we celebrate all of them in ways we hope our son will one day teach his children. One thing we do every time — and so do many covens here, and so does TAWN — is collect food for our Community Food Bank. We've printed up some cards *(see illustration)* to slip into the boxes we deliver, to let people know who's making the donation and the Sabbat it honors.

Yule

When 'dancer and I were growing up, Christmas was the same every year. Times have changed, though, and our Yules are a little different every year. We do keep some traditions, and we're developing a repertoire of variations on cherished themes. A bright 13-inch tree that my aunt decorated for us with Mexican paper flowers, straw birds, and other tiny treasures comes out every year. So does the fondly remembered "fairy spinner" that chimes delicately when its small candles turn the whirler.

For the Explorer's first Yule, we bought him a stocking we found at a craft fair, appliqued with a cloth elf that looked just like the boy. We still have it, but we don't use it anymore because now we use little *cauldrons* instead of

Soon to be victorious, the Explorer helps to re-enact the annual mid-winter battle between the Oak King and the Holly King as Uncle Bilbo watches.

stockings. I bought several little cauldrons, 8 inches at the mouth, at an after-Halloween sale one year, and I fill them with "stocking stuffers."

Some presents go under the tree, but a good many of them are piled up in one of the two big plastic (sorry) cauldrons we have. We open the presents from the little cauldron(s) before breakfast, recalling one of my family's traditions; the rest we open in Circle at Cakes and Ale. (By the way, we use non-alcoholic "ales.")

Every year we save the trunk of the Yule tree, cutting it into logs (only a couple of inches in diameter, but still logs) that we can use to start other Sabbat fires, including the next Yule fire, if the Weber's not rained out. One year we found a Yule-log cake at a French bakery, and I was so excited I paid $9 for it without batting an eye. Now we're keeping our eyes open for a specialty pan in which to bake our own Yule-log cakes!

Brigid (Imbolc, Bride)

We love candles, even if they do curl the cats' eyebrows! So at Bride, the ritual might be short but the candles are tall and burn all evening, filling the house with light and warmth like the returning Sun's.

We do like to dress a Biddy and decorate a Wand in a rite modified from the Farrars' in *A Witches Bible Compleat.* We don't grow our own wheat, so we can't braid the Biddy from the last sheaf of harvest. We use raffia, which the cats appreciate. (Maybe it makes up for curled eyebrows.)

We notice the lengthening hours of light, and on some days it's even warm enough to open the front door in the afternoon. Most years we leave some of our Yule garlands up for a few weeks, but in keeping with traditions older than ours, we take them down at Brigid.

The custom of removing Yule's fragrant greenery from the house at Imbolc clears away the old growth so that Bride's germinations have room to sprout, and our ritual includes a symbolic ramada-sweeping. We start our "spring cleaning" then, too, often with sweet-grass purification. The Explorer takes part in all of this, and with supervision while the smudges are burning, so can your children.

Eostara

Sometimes it's warm enough to camp for Eostara, and we've taken our egg-dying cups with us to color eggs in the woods. We have egg hunts, too, with eggs hidden near sprouting flowers so that whoever finds an egg makes two discoveries. There's always been some gift "from the Equinox," too — a special sighting of wildlife, for instance, or spectacular pictures that surprise us when we have the film developed.

You can take your eggs and dye to a local park or out in the yard. If using real eggs for a hunt is impractical, you can use the plastic ones that come apart; try filling them with runes on colored paper. You can hide decorative wooden eggs, too, or cut some from construction paper.

The stores are full of Easter cards and decorations. All the little girls in the neighborhood are frilled up in new pink and purple dresses and shiny white shoes; the little boys are sporting sharp suits with hankies in their pockets. Their mothers dress them up while our Mother dresses up the Earth in leaf and bud.

In some areas of the country, Eostara would be almost as subtle as Imbolc but for the mainstream's Easter

In the enchanting Chiricahua Mountains of southeastern Arizona, Campsight Coven hosts a five-day Beltane celebration annually, dancing the Maypole without a hitch! (Photo © 1991 by Al Bond)

festivities. This is a great time to talk about history, about fertility and rebirth, the youth of the year and the growth to come. With older children and cowan family and friends, Eostara can be an appropriate time to explore a variety of religious metaphors and symbolism. Thoughts as well as baby chicks can be hatched!

Beltane

Our Maypole lives in our ramada, giving it a cheerful air (kind of romantically medieval, I think). When we go out to camp, last year's ribbons stream behind us, over the wreath of flowers on the spare tire.

We exchange presents at Beltane as well as at Yule, so our Blazer, its antenna sporting mini-ribbons, is fully loaded with gifts as well as with camping gear. We're not extravagant — our presents are usually things we can play with, toy boats and kites and the like. One year we all got specially imprinted sweatshirts; at 6,000 feet, it's still chilly even by Beltane!

We have favorite Maypole music that we play every year on our portable "boom box." *Music from the Hearts of Space*, broadcast on the "classical station," is our main source of Sabbat music. We play lots of specifically pagan music, too, but when the need is for something instrumental, we often use "space music." One year, though, we had a bagpiper, and that was better than anything!

We dress up a little for the Maypole in long skirts, tunics, and garlands in our hair — one year the Explorer wore a wizard's hat. And yes, the Great Rite has been performed, for the woods where we go are both sacred and private.

What we try to do at Beltane, while we're removed from the city's concerns and can live in our Mother's house for a few days, is recreate a sense of old community. We become a little village of tents (some owned, some rented or borrowed; ours is named May Hall); a little Circle of hearth fires.

We have to chop wood and carry water and work at our comfort, just like in the old times. We have at least one communal feast; every year we have a stone soup to which everyone contributes a little something. And there's always a bonfire, a real one, to sing and leap!

Litha

If we camp, our ritual is low key and varies to take advantage of the wild space where we pitch our tent. If we're in town, we keep the Sabbat with other Tucson Witches in a public park.

Not all of us have children, of course, nor are all our children the same age. But camping or in town, everybody cares for all the kids, giving them time, attention, and affection, sharing our Wiccan values, showing them our joy.

In 1990 CE, one of Tucson's very gifted Priestesses, a young mother, introduced a wonderful new element to the ritual — the Sun Pole. It rose out of the "Christmas tree" stand from the middle of a circle of 50 of us, and we hung tokens of our joy upon it. One woman hung a feather, symbolic of the freedoms she gave up to be a mommy and the freedoms she enjoys in motherhood. The ceremony moved many of us to tears, and is sure to be repeated in years to come.

We are celebrating abundance, full strength, "the prime," at Litha, when everything is at its height. Yet our appreciation of the height is only possible from an awareness of depth. A re-enactment of the Oak and Holly Kings' semi-annual battle, Holly victorious and reigning till Yule, keeps things in perspective. Children lend an appropriately gleeful confidence, battling with wrapping-paper-tube swords and full-throated cries of sheer aliveness.

Lughnassad

My office is in an old Victorian house with a big yard, and on one of the fences grows a vine. Someone told me once that it's Bleeding Heart; appreciating irony as I do, I hope that's right! Every year I make a Vine God from it.

Sometime in late June, I take two large paper cups and tape the open ends together. Then (on a lunch hour) I go outside, and after asking nicely and saying thanks, I cut some long strands of vine and start winding. I make a loop for the head, and I usually make horns, too (although we sometimes have to take it on faith that they are horns). The arms and legs are easy.

I dry Him on a shelf in my office. Every year I write a little note of explanation:

> *In case you're wondering, this is a Vine God. He represents the grain and fruit that nourish us all. At the first Harvest Festival, around the first of August, we will fill Him with cornbread and then let Him die on a fire, as fruits and grain ripen every year and die in the harvest so that we can live. When the Vine God has been consumed, the cornbread will be left, and we will share it in a communion honoring life's cycles.*

Vine God

The people I work with are Catholic, Protestant, and Jewish, and they are always interested and respectful.

When it's time, I take the Vine God home; sometimes we get a ride home with 'dancer, and sometimes He rides on the bus with me. On Lammas Night, 'dancer makes a special dinner, different every year but for the cornbread, and strawberries if we can get them.

You can make a Vine God, too, and fill Him with foil-wrapped cornbread — there's a place for it in the middle, where the paper cups were. Watch Him go up in the proverbial blaze of glory on your Weber bonfire. When He is gone, like grain from the fields and fruit from the branches, unwrap the cornbread, bless it, and share it. At dinner afterwards, talk about the harvest and how it works in the Worlds and your lives.

Mabon

Tucson's annual and public *Fall Festival and Faire*, sponsored by the Tucson Area Wiccan Network, attracts more than 200 people, our family circle among them. It's a "cauldron-luck," and a real community celebration of the harvest. Everyone brings the kids, and until it's time for the ritual, we all have to look out for frisbees and footballs!

In 1990 CE, we collected over 100 pounds of food and a lot of cash for the Community Food Bank. When 'dancer took in the boxes, he found the Food Bank workers knew of TAWN and were glad to have a donation from Tucson's Witches.

We think it's important to do public ritual for several reasons. It lets our son realize that what we do is not just a family tradition, but a world-wide human tradition. When he sees 200 people from all over Southern Arizona come together in a public park, it's easier for him to accept that there are Gatherings like this in other cities, too.

At the Fall Festival, he sees the many traditions of Wicca, and some outward expressions and symbols — coven banners, Earth flags, drums, dress robes and the like. And in the huge ritual Circle, he can get some feel for the great Sabbats of old, when hundreds of Witches, coveners and solitaires, gathered to observe our Rites in Common.

That's not to mention the good that public ritual does for Wicca's public image. The Fall Festival at Mabon doesn't have to compete with other public holidays, and with "Halloween" coming up, our openness helps sensitize people. It also makes the sometimes thankless task of public education a lot more fun.

At home, if there's time to relax, we like to weave Cords of Life, something we learned from Starhawk's Mabon ritual in *The Spiral Dance*. We don't get a chance to do that every year, but the Cords from years past hang in the ramada and remind us to consider our personal harvests every year.

Samhain

Faerie Moon and the Norseman host a secular costume party every year, and we love to dress up and go. And every year, we host the religious ritual here at the covenstead. We like to hold it on the 31st, weekend or not, and at midnight if we can. (To this end, I usually take the day after Halloween off from work and the Explorer stays home from school.)

Every year we hope to camp for Samhain. There are lots of really great ritual sites in Southeastern Arizona, and we know of some that are particularly effective. Camping in cold weather — and having a good time at it — requires careful planning, and some years we just can't get it together.

When a seriously primal Samhain is possible, well, it's better to fall upon the sword than to enter that Circle with fear in your heart. There is nothing like a dark, chilly and unfamiliar environment — one you know is physically safe — to give you a head start on understanding what Samhain is all about. The scariest movies and commercial haunted houses pale by comparison, and it's just about the most fun a Witch can ever have!

The Explorer enjoys holiday muffins and non-alcoholic "ale" during a Samhain ritual.

We light candles for our dead, and emphasize Nature's demonstrations that all of life is part of the cycle and comes back. One of the readings we like to include — or it can be sung — is called "In the Cycles of the Planet." I wrote it several years ago, and it goes like this:

> *In the cycles of the planet*
> *dwell our human lives and spirits:*
> *in the patterns on the Water,*
> *in the rhythms of the Sun.*
> *In the Air that we are breathing*
> *hangs the story of our future;*
> *in the heartbeat of the Earth,*
> *we hear the course our lives will run.*
> *So for all the spirits living*
> *in our work and in our memories,*
> *we gather now to sing the songs*
> *of darkness and of light.*
> *For those who've gone before us,*
> *oh, we sing of how we miss them;*
> *and for those who've yet to join us,*
> *we sing welcoming tonight!*

As above, so below. The constellations are not stationary in our skies, nor are they erratic. No, they cycle 'round and 'round, rolling with the seasons. So do we. You can't create or destroy energy; that's the first law of physics, and it holds true for all energy. From a Wiccan perspective, this means it's reasonable to expect that the energy released by death will be transformed to new life.

Beyond death, I give peace, and freedom, and reunion with those who have gone before, the Goddess promises. Commonly, we understand "those who have gone before" to mean people we know who have died, but "those who have gone before" are also those loved ones who have "gone" back to the physical plane. In the Summerland or reincarnated, we believe with many other Wiccans that "reunion" means a joining with all the family groups we have built through the many generations.

So we're beginning to tell family stories, ancestral stories, at Samhain. The veil is thin now, and not only between the Worlds. The distinctions between past and present fade, between tribe and nuclear family. When all the ancestors come to Samhain's family reunion, those of us incarnate at the moment feel the nurturing embrace of all our generations, and it is just as warm as the Sun in high Summer.

As the Explorer gets older and develops a more complete understanding of the relationships between metaphor and "reality," we'll introduce divining, as Samhain is traditionally a time for *sight*. In the meantime, we focus on Samhain as a family reunion, a new year, and the God's descent into the Underworld as a concept/ion and gestation, and consider what we will bring from the harvest to the rebirth at Yule.

The Practical Side

In addition to marking the Sabbats religiously, we observe them practically, too. In Arizona, the Sun dominates our lifestyle. His course through the year determines when we open which blinds and what windows to take best advantage of the weather.

I notice the differences even at the bus stop: between Beltane and Samhain, I don't need a coat! The shadow of the bus stop sign moves about five feet along the ground from Yule to Litha. And of course, the Explorer can play outside longer. By Litha it's light until almost ten in the evening, and that's without daylight savings!

These are things that every family can notice. Even if you can't observe the Sabbats with Wicca's full religious glory, you can take a nature walk through your neighborhood. You can go to the planetarium; if there isn't one where you live, there's likely to be one at the closest university, and it might be worth going the four times a year that most planetariums put on seasonal shows. You can visit local museums, botanical gardens and libraries, too. All of them will have relevant shows sometime.

A project that can be interesting for children and adults is making a Wheel of the Year. It can be as simple or elaborate as your tastes and budget run. On nature walks, or when you're at the park or camping, you can pick up leaves, small rocks and twigs, feathers, and other souvenirs of the wild. From colorful magazine pages or construction paper you can cut out other symbols of the Sabbats. With an inexpensive bottle of glue, you can fasten these things to a Wheel you've made with string, yarn, or construction paper and pasted to a piece of poster board or length of material.

Among other things you might use on such a Wheel are pictures of clouds and other weather symbols cut out of the paper or magazines, small shells, bells, ribbons, tiny paper chains, silk leaves and blossoms, etc. In the middle, you might like to use drawings you or your children have made of the Goddess and the God.

The Wheel you make will be a fine backdrop to your altar. It's an excellent teaching device as well, for you can use it to show your kids (and remind yourself) of the relationships between the seasons and our holidays. And in its making, you'll learn a lot about the way the seasons affect your lives. You'll be reminded that seasons are not

The Explorer shows off the Coven's Green Man, created from a glittery full-face mask and silk leaves to hang near the altar at indoor and outdoor Sabbats.

our invention, but like the grain and game that die annually, were here long before we humans grew up, and will be here when we have all been transformed.

As your Wheel of the Year becomes an heirloom, its corners bent, its decorations re-glued a hundred times, it will become a symbol of the Gods Themselves. Though the decorations and pictures you've made it with may tear and fold and fade, the Wheel itself remains, reborn with every new illustration, every new decoration, every loving repair. Just so are we renewed in every cycle, transformed every day.

Don't forget food, either. Like cowan families, we have special foods for holidays. Children can help from young ages, and special Sabbat recipes can become treasured family heirlooms. We like to vary the holiday menu from year to year; whether you like to repeat your repasts or not, there are many sources of festive pagan recipes.

Try Scott Cunningham's *The Magic in Food*, published by Llewellyn in 1991, and Helen Farias' *Octava/The Beltane Papers*, a newsletter from the Pacific Northwest (Post Office Box 8, Clear Lake, Washington, 98235). Many other fine sources are available, of course: check your own bookshelves, your catalogues — maybe even your local paper!

Deck the Halls!

Most families like to decorate for the holidays; we usually do our house and our car. But finding Wiccan decorations can be a challenge, even if we can use many of the same garlands and ornaments that everyone else does.

We've found that right after Christmas, there are a lot of Beltane decorations on sale, although the stores selling them at half-price or less probably don't know that's what they are! Lights and tinsel in a variety of colors are marked down, and so are ornaments, many of which are suitable for Beltane, Litha, and even Eostara. The cottony white squares decorated with multi-colored glitter sold for Christmas tree skirts make fine Maypole skirts, too.

Bells, colored glass balls, stars (occasionally penta-grams!) and faeries (they call them angels) — all of these, along with bead and "evergreen" garlands, are appropriate to several of our holidays. Even those things which are too Yule-ish to use any other time can be used in ways the cowan would never imagine: candle wreaths of silk fir, pine or holly, for example, make great crowns for battling Kings. If you go to a five-and-dime or a craft store after Christmas, Easter and Halloween, you'll find lots of decorations and accessories for the Sabbats.

We like to make decorations, too. We make paper chains every Yule (kittens really like them!). At Eostara we decorate eggshells, which we can then string or hang by pipe cleaners. We've used wrapping paper tubes to make miniature Maypoles; decorated with tin foil or colored paper and ribbons, they're just right for Oak and Holly Kings' swords, too.

With ribbons and other pretty scraps and a block of florists' foam or styrofoam shapes that any craft store carries, even a small child can make a nice centerpiece or headpiece. Putting the decoration in a small cauldron and tying the cauldron with a bright ribbon will brighten up a table, mantle, or corner at any Sabbat.

A larger cauldron will hold a punchbowl, too, and decorated with a bow or other ornaments, it's a neat way to serve up any brew. (At Samhain, of course, you'll want to add dry ice.) You might be able to stand a Maypole or a small Yule tree in a large cauldron, as well. Our "Christmas tree stand" holds the Maypole as well as a Yule tree, every year.

Faerie Moon found a six-foot twig broom at a craft store, and it stands, bristles up, of course, by her massive stone fireplace. She decorates it with tiny colored lights and seasonal baubles. Everyone loves it! You can make a Yule broom if you don't choose to use a real or artificial tree. We use a white-painted and be-ribboned broom to mark the site of our annual Beltane, too.

Do we have to wait for a Sabbat to decorate? Not at all! We don't even have to wait for birthdays, anniversaries, graduations, passages, our teams' championships, or company, either. Our homes can be festive year 'round.

Winter is cold even in Arizona, and houses can be drafty. In "the old days," tapestries and other wall hangings blunted the chill — they can today, too! You can hang a wall with quilts or curtains or even area rugs. Brick veneer or real wood paneling can evoke the feeling of ancestral halls.

Fireplaces can be decked with seasonal garlands or bouquets; mantles can be subtle altars, for many a mantle figure (museum reproductions, for instance) is pagan. Charms can be disguised as mainstream crafts, if disguise is necessary, and displayed on a mantle, bookshelf or table.

If you know your ethnic heritage, you can bring it home in your choice of furniture styles and colors. "Regional" colors here include a forest green, common as well to Celtic decoration. We enjoy being able to conjure up our own cultural heritage, keeping right in vibrant Southwest style at the same time!

There are color choices even for apartment walls, and one thing almost anyone can do is coordinate wall colors with quarter colors. (We don't recommend painting each wall of a room a different color! But three walls neutral and one wall a directional color can be nice.)

Windows can be decorated, not merely covered, with curtains — and they're easy to make. The clerks at most fabric stores will help you, or you can get one of many how-to books. All you really need is to be able to sew a straight seam. Wreaths and garlands are nice on windows, too.

Tablecloths are easy to make as well. For most rectangular kitchen tables, all you need is two yards of any fabric you like. Cut 12 inches off one end — cut that strip in quarters and you have four napkins, or leave it long and you have a runner or an altar cloth. The napkins or runner and the large piece just need narrow hemming. The tablecloth only needs hemming on the two short ends; the long sides are selvage edges and can be left as they are. These tablecloths can be inexpensive enough to make one for every Sabbat and another for Moons, if you want.

They're just the right size to completely cover a 48-quart cooler, too, turning it into a portable altar with storage space for tools and the cakes and ale, as long as you don't mind a chilled handle on your athame. I've used the cloth-covered cooler as an altar for the rituals I sometimes demonstrate to local church groups, and it works better than a cardboard box.

Archways and interior doors are good places for curtains, swags or garlands, and doors take posters — or paint. In the bathroom, you have the same freedom with shower curtains as you do with tablecloths — you can make your own, with any fabric you like. Measure the curtain bar, and add 18 inches to the measurement. Measure the length from the curtain bar to the floor, and add three inches. Then do some figuring — how much material you'll need depends on the fabric width. You'll have to sew a center seam to get a piece big enough, and you'll need extra fabric to match plaids or other such patterns.

The edges will be selvage, and won't need a hem. At the top and bottom, begin with a 1½-inch hem. At the top, through both layers of fabric, make 12 buttonholes, evenly spaced. If you have a sewing machine, it may have a buttonholer. Otherwise I think grommets will work, but be sure first that the ones you choose are big enough to fit over the hooks on your shower curtain rings. The bottom hem should fall somewhere between a quarter of an inch to an inch above the floor.

The only other thing you'll need is a clear plastic shower curtain to line it. Your new fabric curtain stays outside the tub at all times, while the plastic one stays inside. Shower curtains, like window curtains, are pretty easy to make, and they'll do wonders for your bathroom's mood — and your family's. If your bathroom has a window, you can make matching curtains; sometimes it's okay to be a "designer Witch."

Another way to decorate your house no matter what the season is with the "mini-lights" they sell for the Winter holidays. You can hang crystals in your windows, too, or paint delicate designs on the edges and in the corners with tempera paints. (This is a wonderful family project for sliding glass doors at the Sabbats, or on an inclement or recovering-from-something afternoon, and clean-up isn't too bad.)

Coven banners are great fun to make, and your coven doesn't have to be large — or rich — to hang one. The Wiccan community here is fairly public, so we see banners at most gatherings; the Tucson Area Wiccan Network has one, too, that flies every month at the "cauldron-luck" in the park.

Faerie Moon and I were at a store that sells fabric by weight when we found the oversized sample squares that became the field for Campsight's banner. I sewed four of them — same pattern, different colors — together for the background, which measures about two feet by four feet.

In the center we wanted an obvious symbol of Witch-craft, and decided on a cauldron. I cut a large one out of black cotton, leaving a collar-like edge at the top. I put a circle of batting down, and a smaller one on top of it, so the cauldron is in soft bas-relief. Over a narrow strip of batting, I rolled the cauldron's collar down so that it has the depth of a real cauldron's rim. I have a sewing machine, and used it to sew down the bowl of the cauldron, but I finished the rim by hand.

An arching arrangement of "silk" leaves and branches is sewn above the cauldron. The greenery extends just about an inch beyond the sides of the banner so the leaves can move and rustle softly in the breeze.

Below the cauldron is a triple Moon, cut from a flex-ible mirror-like material. The two crescents and the full circle are glued down; they are also edged with glittery fabric paint. The Explorer made the choice of "rainbow" glitter from among several colors.

Beneath all the symbols and decorations are the words CAMPSIGHT COVEN spelled out on two centered lines. The let-ters are wooden, from a local craft store, painted black and edged with metallic copper. Copper is not an especially tra-ditional Wiccan material, but it is a traditional material here in the Southwest and becoming popular elsewhere.

The beads on the end of the three foot-long black dowel on which the banner hangs are glued in place, and are brushed with copper, too. We have a length of purple

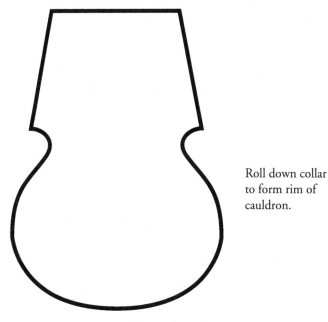

Roll down collar
to form rim of
cauldron.

Pattern for cauldron

leather cord by which to hang it. In the house, the dowel rests on two nails and we don't need the hanging cord, but in the park or the woods, we can't always find two branches close enough and level, so the cord comes in handy.

The finished banner was dedicated when we formalized the Coven. But before it was officially consecrated, it was made with Celtic music — Gwyddion Pendragon, mostly — playing to it in the background. While I was absorbed in the hand-work, the banner went with my imagination to the hills of Ireland, Scotland and Wales, waving over leprechaun and fairy feasts. It holds its own magic as well as the dedication we gave.

The Explorer was somewhat indifferent about the banner while I was making it. (The project took up most of the back room and my time for a few evenings.) But now that it's done, he's as proud of it as we are!

So don't wait to decorate! The spirit is with us all the time — the God greets us every morning, the Goddess every evening. They do so much to make the world homey for us that we enjoy making our little corner homey for Them.

If we aren't limited to decorating on special occasions, are we limited to our houses and yards? Certainly not! When we camp on a holiday, Campsight decorates the woods as well! We hang banners and garlands and streamers — on our tents, from the cars, from low branches. Sometimes we make rice-paper chains, and we have cut stars and spirals from dried seaweed to decorate the ground, and we can leave our decorations to feed the feathers and furries.

ELF-LIGHTS

Several years ago, Faerie Moon created what she calls *elf-lights,* and camping by ourselves or together, we've used them ever since. To tell you how to make your own, here's Faerie Moon herself, excerpted from the Aprés-Eostara, 1990 CE issue of *The Celtic Camper,* our quarterly newsletter.

I easily recall the first one I built while we were camped on the edge of a huge meadow in the White Mountains. Dinner was barely finished when the dark started to bubble forth a summer storm. My husband hustled about securing things, and I began to fret about how to save the pretty votive candles I had flickering at the boundaries of our camp.

The moist wind was threatening to snuff them, and suddenly I began to bank the closest votive with some handy flat, fist-sized rocks. Stacking them so that odd gaps allowed the colored light through, I capped the top of the little cairn with one long, slender piece of rock to fully shield the flame.

Inspired, I rushed to do the same for about four other votives. Luckily, plenty of rocks were available, and the ground had been cleared of flammable wisps of grass beforehand. The storm finally hit, dousing two of the lights; but the remaining ones shone bravely throughout! The rain was soon over, leaving an intoxicating damp green scent from the meadow. I relit the damaged votives and my husband and I settled back to enjoy the sensations.

After a few moments, my husband focused on the nearest stone cairn I had decorated with a couple of pine cones. "So, just what do you call these?" he asked, interested.

"Elf-lights," I answered before really thinking, although by instinct (Irish ancestry here) I knew that was what I had spontaneously built.

"What are they for?" My husband naturally asked this because he has learned that when Witches do such things, they usually mean something.

"Well, besides the fact that they keep us from tripping over the dark parts of our camp," I answered a bit smugly, "they form a protective area that invites the Wee Folk to come and bless our visit here in their home. Sort of a respectful beacon, you might say."

Some are simple cairns for single votive candles, but some elf-lights become elf-castles, like this one holding five candles and decorated with courtyards and crystals as well as with pine cones and flowers.

Then we started to go camping with O'Gaea and Canyon-dancer and their son. Our first time out, I instructed them to gather many rocks (the flatter and more stackable, the better) and we began a tradition with them that continues to this day.

With more folks helping, the elf-lights got fancier in spots, some nestled in rocks over water, lit up like diminutive caves once the sun sank down. Others were placed in gnarled root grottos (carefully shielded with stones so as not to catch fire). Some were decorated with seasonal offerings, statues of gnomes, or given tiny crystal windows when we wedged clear quartz pieces in amongst the stones.

If you'd like to try elf-light building (inside your home or out), there are a few important guidelines. The most important, of course, is safety: i.e., fire hazard. Some campgrounds, especially those patrolled by rangers, have strict fire codes, and you could be fined for any "open flame" outside your campfire.

Don't build where there's abundant dry grass or flammable dry branches. Clear elf-light circumferences down to dirt, and select broad, flat stones for a fire-proof base for your votive candle *in a glass holder.* Then insulate the light, building up on all sides with rocks. Be cautious with decorations near the flame; make sure nothing can accidentally fall or blow in and catch fire.

Always use slats of thin rock to cap the cairn, several inches above the flame, for extra protection. Stagger the wall-rocks enough so the light will show through — and experiment with different colored glasses for different colors of light!

Be innovative as well as practical in placing elf-lights; they make excellent path markers, and of course, beautiful celebratory touches for your indoor facilities. Permanent elf-lights can be erected in your own yard; they can be cemented in place, leaving the cap stone(s) loose for candle placement.

I've gone on Moon walks with several other Witches, and we've made elf-lights to sit around and exchange stories or songs. These cozy little cairns provide an ancient pagan link to the days of old, and are perfect to mark the directions when summoning Elementals. I even had them in my wedding circle!

So try elf-lights, and sit back to watch the Wee Folks creep up next to the glittering mounds of stones. And always remember what Smokey (the obviously pagan Bear) says: Be careful with fire. Blesséd be, Campers!

When we've finished our elf-lights, we build other things from twigs, bundles of pine needles, rocks, and fallen cones. We build castles and lodges, often softly telling the stories that go with them. (Stories are decorations too, of the mind and of the spirit.) If there's wild water about — usually a small, rocky stream — we'll build pine cone boats and rafts to sail in it. Stories come with them, too, and here's one of them!

The Antlered Oak Boat of Upper Herrin

Upper Herrin was so called to be distinguished from Herrin, which was an abandoned fishing village on the Grey Rock River. The Grey Rock River was so called because its course was lined with grey rocks, some of them pearly, some of them dark and time-smoothed.

It is not always necessary to build boats to fish from in a river; if your river is swift and narrow, it would be suicidal. Upper Herrin was about a mile upstream from Herrin, and farther than that from suicidal. It was a comfortable community, growing more and more wealthy from increasing enterprise. Upper Herrin did not need to build fishing boats, Upper Herrin needed to build tourist boats.

It was too dangerous to sail boats in the gorge along which Upper Herrin was built. But it was perfectly safe to moor boats permanently in the shoals to feed, house and enter-tain tourists who came to see the quaint lifestyle of Upper Herrin, where they'd heard people lived in permanently moored boats.

To maintain tourist interest, Upper Herrin began to discover and share its history. Even though they made most of it up, one or two accuracies slipped by them. One of these accidental accuracies was a story that long, long ago, when old Herrin itself had been a mere circle of huts and a stick altar, Herriners had been hunters.

A dreadful fire in one season followed by an incomparably cold winter threatened them all. To save the people, the Horned One appeared to them as an enchanted hart, fully new-antlered at entirely the wrong time to be fully antlered. He led the astonished hunters to the river bank, where to their further astonishment, the hart strode into the water and bellowed a single note.

His voice called, from one of the river-side oaks, a tremendous shudder, and a large branch plummeted to the ground, striking the magical hart dead between the eyes. The hart's body then transformed itself, and what the stunned hunters saw at the end of their watching was an antlered leather boat with an oaken mast.

(Water-logged bundles of pine needles, braided and woven around the ends of twigs, were the "leather" of the rafty boat I held in my hands; such transformation is, of course, not beyond the Horned One.)

So it was by this magical boat that the old Herriners were carried up the stream, and their rafts of belongings were pulled behind it to the place that became Upper Herrin. Generations later, finding their living so easy to make in the abundance to which the God had led them, they had quite a lot of leisure time, which they filled first by constructing a studio complex on a nearby outcropping *(represented on this camping trip by a rather elaborate elf-light)*, and after that by doing crafts.

One day a honeymooning couple from a foreign land picnicked near the Grey Rock River, and hearing fragments of song and smelling fragments of delicious cooking, came on until they found the town of Upper Herrin. They went wild with delight and spent so much money buying Upper Herrin crafts that the only way they were able to dine on the rest of their honeymoon was to sit near other people and ask them if they were going finish *that,* pointing to whatever looked good.

When that couple returned to the place they came from, along with settling down and raising a family (which they did but which doesn't concern us here, although they did lead interesting lives and their second daughter led an even more interesting life than that), they showed all their friends the things they had bought in Upper Herrin, and told them all how to get there.

After that, Upper Herrin saw a lot of visitors from a lot of foreign lands, and through the eager exchange of crafts for an assortment of currencies, Upper Herrin became more sophisticated and flourished. The pace at last became so hectic that the economy slowed down. After a few years, the hope and effort to revitalize was desperate; and that was when the addition of an historical dimension to Upper Herrin's tourist trade was seen to be effective, and everyone, almost, contributed to Upper Herrin's collected history.

Fictions, fireside stories, fantasy and fact were given equal credit, and the best bits were illustrated. The story of the Antlered Oak Boat of Upper Herrin, suspected to be fantasy, was entirely true. And by a coincidence that would have been as astounding to Upper Herriners as the magical hart had been to their ancestors, this model of the Antlered Oak Boat of Upper Herrin is absolutely accurate, too.

A story like this is a blessing, too. A twig-and-pine-cone boat that sails on a stream in the woods — or across the wading pool you inflate for the kids — may not need much of a blessing, but it can't hurt. When our elf-lights get elaborate — I remember one I built from white rocks in a little plateau between two gnarled roots of a tree that overhung our campsite — we sometimes tell their stories, and then we can call upon the power of the story to bless the light and the site.

As I sit at the computer, my left brain makes me smile at this thought, but when I'm in the woods under dappled sunlight, breathing the pines' natural incense with the feel of real earth beneath my feet, I know it's true: there are Little People living in the folk tales we tell as well as in the woods, and when we do them the honor of a story's acknowledgement, they are very generous with their blessings in return.

TOOLS AND ACCESSORIES

The Sabbats (and to a lesser extent, Esbats) are often more fun to celebrate when a variety of tools and accessories are available. Our Yules, for instance, wouldn't be nearly so much fun without the cardboard swords the Oak and Holly Kings so colorfully swing. A wide and elegant variety of accessories are available from many stores and catalogues, but they're not always within our budget, and because it just doesn't do to haggle over the cost of ritual accessories, we sometimes need to find other sources.

Check out your local thrift shops; you'll find all kinds of wonderful things in your favorite second-hand stores. The Goddess figure that stands under the North altar in our yard is a hand-made ceramic piece, an eclectic combination of Maiden, Mother and Crone — and we found Her at Value Village for $1.50! Until She disintegrated and "returned to Herself," we had a straw Maiden from the thrift shop, and we're delighted to know that an identical one stands on a shelf in the Explorer's school library!

I've found tarnished but gorgeous brass and copper chalices at thrift shops, and censors with handles. Candles, sometimes so overpriced, are sold for just pennies each — and not only tapers, columns or votives, either. For next Beltane I have a three-sided pink flower candle about four inches in diameter, and saved from last Beltane, a garlanded Unicorn.

If you want to make God-robes (for Samhain, for instance), and you'd like to use real fur without being an environmental bad guy, head to the thrift shop. There you'll find fur coats that you can pick up for pennies on the dollar of their original cost, and you'll be rescuing their spirits when you remake them into ritual robes. The fur that trims our coven's antlered headpiece comes from a collar I bought at a thrift shop for about $2.00!

Maiden's, Mother's and Crone's dresses sometimes appear on thrift-shop racks, too. We've found wonderful shawls and other cape-like wraps as well. On tablecloth racks we've found nice altar cloths, some hand-woven or embroidered. Now and again, something suitable to wrap cards or other tools shows up. Chosen carefully, hand-washed and consecrated, these things can become a family's or a coven's heirlooms.

Some years ago I used an old choir robe from the thrift shop when as part of a presentation I dressed up as a fairy-tale Witch, complete with green-faced mask. After I ran around the assembled listeners, cackling stereotypically so they would recognize the character, I doffed both mask and robe to reveal the real Witch underneath.

The old choir robe was easy to get off, and suffered no disrespect even though it got kicked around a little when we danced the Spiral later. You could use a similar act at a Halloween party to introduce your child's friends (or yours) to Wicca, too.

The truth is, I buy virtually all my clothes, and some of Canyondancer's and the Explorer's, at the thrift shop. It saves money, sure, but it's also an act of community and it's a significant form of recycling, too. No matter what I buy at any of the several thrift shops I frequent, I know I'm helping the planet as well as myself.

7

PASSAGES

We recognize few passages in this culture; coming of age means you can go out to a bar. Deep down, most of us expect better. The passage into adulthood is one of the most important we can manage. It's important to humans to get some guidance, feedback and approval.

Passage rituals reassure us, help us consolidate our confidence and courage to press onward; as life does, as the God does. Celebrating our own passages is part of celebrating the Wheel of the Year, for we are the God: we die and are reborn, and our journey 'round each time is sacred.

Our family/coven recognizes several passages in a life, and we even have rituals for some of them! For us, birth, Wiccaning, one or more dedications and a recognition of puberty pave the way for Initiations; then there are Queenings and Kingings, Cronings and Sagings, and finally, deathing and Requiems.

It would be nice to have ritual celebrations of conceptions, and perhaps on the anniversary of a death, a ritual to reaffirm our faith in reincarnation. As our family/coven grows, perhaps such rituals will be added to our Book of Shadows; in the meantime, we'll share some of the rituals we do have.

BEGINNINGS

Blessing from the East

When I was asked to call East at the Wiccaning of a friend's baby, here is what I said:

> *Hail, Guardians in the East, starseekers, whirlwinds! By the Air that is Her breath, I ask your blessings on our Circle and your light upon our work. So mote it be! You are latest come among us, but not least, and in token of your welcome, I bring blessings from the East.*

A small crystal affixed to a jewelry-type pin was bestowed upon the child at this point, with her father's help.

> *May you always think clearly,*
> *May you always trust the spring;*
> *You will always be loved dearly —*
> *May love always make you sing!*
> *May you always be beginning,*
> *May you always keep the feasts;*
> *And while the Spiral's spinning,*
> *May you be blessèd by the East!*

To dismiss the Quarter, I said:

> *Guardians in the East, starseekers, whirlwinds! We thank you for your blessing and bid you Goddesspeed to go in peace. Blessèd be.*

The Explorer was first dedicated to the Craft when he was seven. We will offer him a second dedication when he is about 14; after that it will be up to him to ask for initiation. We expect to add an initiatory element to his 21st birthday celebration, though, because we think that is appropriate both socially and religiously.

Do we anticipate the Explorer being Wiccan all his life? Yes, we do, and at this point, so does he. We are raising him to a Wiccan understanding of the world. Wicca's major tenets are real for him objectively and subjectively.

If we were answering his questions with inconsistent nonsense, one of these days he'd notice that and reject our teachings. If we prattled on in meaningless clichés, he'd stop paying attention. But we don't. We speak Witchcraft to him, and — very simply — because Witchcraft is true, it won't betray him.

We cannot imagine that the Explorer's life will not affirm Wicca, so we have no hesitation in affirming Wicca to him.

Initial Dedication

This was the Explorer's first "initiation." It took place in our yard, under our ramada, and before we had planted our circle of grass or laid our adobe bricks. Your own yard or a good friend's, a favorite campsite or the family room, will work just as well.

Begin at dusk. In the ramada, some candles are burning. Assembled are more candles, incense, a white cord, a blue cord, a bowl of warm purified water, and a box or pouch.

The young "initiate" is blindfolded and led to the edge of the circle space. There s/he is asked:

> *Do you come to the Circle in perfect love and*
> *perfect trust?*

S/he responds that s/he does.

S/he is then led into the ramada, where his/her hands are washed in the purified water. The white cord is tied around his/her waist and ankle, and s/he is told:

> *Before the Goddess, you are neither bound nor free.*

An initiator's hand is then placed against the "initiate's" chest as s/he faces the North, and s/he is told:

> *You are about to come into a time of special growth*
> *and learning. You will come to know more of*
> *yourself and the world than you can now imagine.*
> *You are about to enter the Circle. Do you have the*
> *courage?*

S/he responds that s/he does.

The "initiate" is then touched by all present, and s/he is blessed as follows:

> *Blesséd be your feet, that walk upon the Earth.*
> *Blesséd be your knees, that kneel at sacred altars.*
> *Blesséd be your potential, that will create life from life.*
> *Blesséd be your breasts, formed in strength.*
> *Blesséd be your lips, that will learn to speak the*
> *sacred words.*

The "initiate" is then measured with the blue cord, which is knotted at each end to mark his/her height from head to heel; his/her head is measured from one knot and another knot is tied; his/her waist is measured from that knot, and a final knot is tied. The "initiate" is then asked:

Are you ready and willing to pledge your mind to learning, your heart to love, your body to life, your life to peace, and your soul to the Goddess?

S/he responds that s/he is.

The knots on the cord are held for him/her to kiss in token of that pledge. The "initiate" then kneels, placing one hand on his/her head and one on his/her heel, and says:

I, _____, pledge that all between my two hands belongs to the Goddess.

Everyone, including the "initiate," says:

So mote it be!

The "initiate's" blindfold is then removed, and the cord is handed to him/her, with these words:

Here is your measure, to remind you of your promise to learn, love, live fully, work for peace, and respect your Mother Earth.

The "initiate" then places the cord into the pouch or box; at this time, the white cord is untied and placed in the pouch or box with the blindfold. The "initiate" is then blessed once more, with water, crystal, incense and flame. The initiator then says:

Mother, behold and bless _____ who today joins the Circle of Your children.

The "initiate" is then hugged and kissed by all present, and everyone goes inside to celebrate.

The Explorer's first initiation and my Call to the East were strongly influenced by Starhawk's rituals. Although we no longer follow them so closely, I am still very fond of them, and we combine favorite parts of them with material from the Farrars' *A Witches Bible Compleat* in our ritual cycle.

CELEBRATIONS

The rituals we've made for the wild sites we love have been some of the most dramatic and powerful we've experienced. These are rites not for our chronological biochemical passages through the physical plane, but for our passages between the Worlds, which we sometimes take for granted.

When we cast our Circles, it is rarely in sheer celebration of being able to step between the Worlds. But this capacity is worth celebrating, and that passage is important. Children of all ages enjoy these rites, too. Younger ones simply immerse themselves in the delight and mystery; older kids can personalize the framework of each such ritual with their own experience.

Not wanting to make any mistakes in the first circle his grandparents (not visible) have ever joined, the Explorer checks his order of service before he purifies the Quarters with a sage-and-lavender smudge. (Photo © 1992 by William B. Law)

It helps to be in the woods, away from cynical city walls, where nature's belief in magic can strengthen ours. But what really makes these rituals glow is that they are purely joyful. Sometimes we work on healing, but more often we simply celebrate Life. All acts of love and pleasure are Her rituals. Camping feels like being in a huge Circle with the Goddess herself High Priestessing, and it is uniquely refreshing to be part of the rituals the Gods perform.

Often, the only Circle around a ritual we do at camp is the horizon of trees and mountains, for the

Guardians do not need to be summoned to their own dwelling places. Sometimes our calling to a place is so strong that it is we who are invoked into the already wholly blessed and sacred sphere.

Campsight has been to southeastern Arizona's Crystal Cave several times. It is one of only three quartz crystal caves in the United States, and though some of the rooms have been stripped by vandals, many of the smaller rooms still glitter in secret. Many a time I have felt, sitting in rooms hardly bigger than geodes, that Merlin was beside me.

Several years ago we were inspired to do the following ceremony, which is half in modern English and "healf" in Anglo-Saxon. The Anglo-Saxon, being somewhat difficult for most of us to pronounce, is written phonetically.

The Ceremony of the Crystal Cave

Onshay thay laikt in oosah yondlickten the shada-helm oosah for-yurdan.

The light within us shall illuminate the many darknesses around us.

Onshay oora ferkth yewit ohv thay oon yedollick en thees yedollick clay-ofa, thot way may onfee thad tha on-yedollicks whella oosah for-yurdath.

In this finite cosm we embrace the several infinities that surround us.

Onshay oora yelled-yekinnd onspringan frome thees forsainlick cars oonder where way standath, thoor oosah ond frome oosah, toe anbywen tha sickth ohv oora sayfas ohn freedness.

Our primal humanity rises from the neglected stones beneath our feet, through us and from us, to clarify the vision of our hearts and minds.

Nima thay strengthoo ohv shadahelm, tha strengthoo ohv seckt ond sailness, ohn way hit habbath mit oosah hereh thees dyeh ond when way gaith froma thees rooma.

We claim the strength of darkness, the strength of peace and silence, and we will have it with us now and when we go from this place.

In tha nahm ohf theh Eortha, befarath en seckt.

In the name of the Earth, we go in peace.

Here's another ritual that is magical, too, in more than one way. It's a reunion with our Source, it's about transformation, emotionally and perceptually, and it is open to a child's or adult's very personal interpretation. Like the *Ceremony of the Crystal Cave,* it both celebrates and facilitates our temporary passages between the Worlds.

We've held this ceremony along a stream that meanders by a clearing near where we camp, the clearing filled with 20 or so elf-lights; sitting by the fire afterwards, Canyondancer said it looked like stars had fallen and lay shining on the ground.

It was an entirely magical, environmental lullaby for the Explorer, who fell asleep watching the lights twinkle through the window in the tent. You can hold this ceremony or one like it in a wading pool in your yard, or even in the bathtub!

Children of the Water

Using styrofoam bowls and tall, clear plastic glasses, make candle boats by gluing the glasses into the bowls and setting votive candles in the glasses. You will also need a chalice filled with your usual ritual drink, and long matches. Purify the "ale," for in this ritual it will be the Water of Life. This ceremony takes place in darkness at stream- or lake-side, but if a domestic pool (decorative or swimming) is what's available, it will do just fine; it would be a good idea to purify captive domestic water first.

Silently, the chalice containing the Water of Life is passed. When all have partaken, say in unison:

> *We are One in the Water of Life. We are One in Life on Earth. We are One.*

Exchange private greetings with the water you are standing beside, and when everyone has done that, say in unison:

> *We are children of the Water; in the Water we are One. From the Water we came to Life; to the Water we come to make our lives whole.*

Now light the candles in the boats, and hold them while you say in unison:

> *In these flames we come home to the Water; in*
> *these lights we offer our dreams to the Water that*
> *gave us Life.*

Now set the candle-boats gently in the water, giving them a gentle push to get them into the current or away from the shore or edge, and say in unison:

> *From the Water we came to Life; to the Water we*
> *come to make our lives whole. In these lights we are*
> *one with the Water. In these lights we are One. We*
> *are children of the Water; in the Water we are One.*

Pass the chalice once more as you watch the candles drift downstream or bob on the water — and don't forget to pick up the candle boats in the morning.

Some passages occur without any religious or cultural acknowledgement, and when that happens, we are subtly disappointed and demoralized. One gift the Wiccan community is giving to our culture is ritual to mark these passages.

Three of us held a Queening ritual one quiet summer weekend in a wood only a couple of hours from Tucson. We got the idea from Z. Budapest's all-in-one *Holy Book of Women's Mysteries,* where she described the need to recognize adulthood, not just sexual maturity, but full-blown adulthood with all its strengths and knowledge.

We decided that a Queening is appropriate for any woman who has achieved her second degree and is at least 35 years old, and who has demonstrated her maturity in attitude and deed. Queening conveys no ecclesiastical rank or privilege, but recognizes the practical, secular authority and dignity of the individual woman and the Wiccan context of her life.

We happened to find lapel buttons that said, YES, YOUR MAJESTY, and we gave those to each other as gifts. We also made "the men" barbecue for us when we came home.

A Queening can be done by a group of women for each other, as ours was, or by friends for one woman. Of course, a Queening can be modified and made a Kinging.

Queening

Gathered in a pleasant place, crowns (and any other accoutrements, including individual chalices or a single chalice of "mead" for all to share) are arranged to the South, for fullness, maturity and bright, shining strength. An altar may be set up; it should be a simple one.

Participants speak *individually* and ***in unison:***

> *When we were little girls, we dreamed of being Queens. Now we make the dream come true.*

> ***Behold, we are women now, and Witches, and the power of dreams is ours.***

> *We are to be crowned Queens: not fearless, but unafraid of fear; not powerful over, but powerful with.*

Each now picks up another's crown and holds it skyward in both hands.

*Behold, we take up these crowns in the name of
the Triple Goddess and the Horned God.*

*We accept the beauty and strength of our maturity,
and claim our crowns with honor and humility.*

*Behold, we charge these crowns with the wisdom
and courage of trust, and with the power and compassion of love.*

Each crowns the woman whose crown she holds, saying as
she places the crown:

I complete your Circle as you complete mine.

Behold, these crowns are . . .

. . .turns of the Spiral,

. . . arcs of the Cauldron's rim,

. . .our curving horizons.

*Behold, these crowns are circlets of sisterhood,
and behold, we are Queens in the sight of Gods
and Witches!*

Now the chalice(s) is/are lifted and the new Queens toast
each other:

Queen _____! Blesséd be!

O'Gaea pours a farewell libation over an offering stone in front of an elf-light built in honor if a friend who died just before Lammas, 1991 CE. (Photo © 1991 by Canyondancer)

After each Queen has been toasted and the chalice(s) drained, each chalice is held aloft. If one is used, all have a hand upon it; if many are used, the bowls are touching.

> *By the Cauldron of Cerridwen, our lives are changing once again! By love and trust we Queens are bound; in these crowns we find our ground. To change with grace and grow in balance: this we pledge, on crown and chalice!*

*With harm to none, our will be done. Queens
and Priestesses are we: as we will, so mote it be!*

Croning and Saging rituals might take similar forms.
You could even do an "Eldering" ritual for a couple. The
passages, physical and metaphysical, that you mark are
yours to choose. From birth to death (cradle to womb, you
might say), there is much to celebrate, and your life's
rituals wait for you to compose them.

A ritual to honor a departed friend can be as simple as
lighting a single candle. For ideas, please see *Eight Sabbats
for Witches* by Janet and Stewart Farrar or *Buckland's Complete Book of Witchcraft.* One of Tucson's most respected,
experienced and well-liked Priestesses, Delia Morgan, has
composed a solitary's Requiem which we like very much
and have entered into our Book of Shadows. She has gra-
ciously given her permission for us to reproduce it here.

Requiem for a Witch

(© Delia Morgan, 1990 CE)

Supplies needed:
Altar with cloth
White taper or pillar candle for the Goddess
Black taper or pillar candle for the God
White votive candle in white container for deceased
Water and salt in dishes
Incense and burner
Vase of flowers
Wand
Small bell
A small black stone

Rosemary ("for remembrance")
Two to three feet of red string or yarn
Small square of paper, and red-inked pen

Set up the altar in the North with flowers at the back, Goddess image and candle on left, Horned God image and candle on right. Arrange other items so as to leave a large space in the middle of the altar. Purify water, bless salt, and mix a pinch of salt into water.

Light white candle and say:

> *Oh, Great Mother Goddess, who gives birth to all that is . . .*

Light black candle and say:

> *Oh, Great Horned God, Lord of death and the Summerland . . .*

Light incense and say:

> *I ask that you be with me tonight and bless this rite.*

Turn deosil in a complete circle and say:

> *Oh, Mighty Ones of the four Quarters — Air and Fire and Water and Earth — I ask that you attend and empower this rite. Bléssed be.*

(It is optional at this point to cast and purify a Circle, purifying yourself with oil, etc.) Say:

Hear ye that _____, a friend and sister in the Craft, has passed beyond the veil.

Ring the bell three times slowly and pause. Say:

Tonight I remember her and honor her spirit as I bid her farewell.

Lay the red string in a spiral on the altar. Say:

She travels now upon the Great Spiral of death and rebirth. Infinite and eternal is the cord which binds us to the Mother Goddess. Night leads to dawn, winter to spring; endless is the Spirit's journey, and ever the Circle shall turn.

Light the votive candle and place it in the middle of the Spiral, and say:

May your spirit be rekindled in new flesh; may you arise in peace.

Lay the black stone to one side of the votive. Say:

I bid you farewell on your journey through the Shadows. May you find peace and rest in the Summerland.

Lay rosemary to the other side of the votive. Say:

You will be remembered in the hearts and minds of those who love you.

Holding the votive candle, circle three times around widdershins to symbolize the journey to the Underworld. Replace the candle in the Spiral.

Face West. Say:

> *You have passed the Western Gateways and set sail upon dark Waters. Fear not, for the Horned One will lead you to the Summerland, and back to the Cauldron of Cerridwen, to be born again of the Great Mother.*

Turn deosil to each of the four Quarters, starting in the West. (West symbolizes dusk, autumn, endings and the Gateway to the Underworld.)

Sprinkle salt water to the West. Say:

> *By the Waters that are Her womb, may you be reborn in love.*

Sprinkle salt to the North. Say:

> *By the Earth that is Her body, may you be reborn in strength.*

Wave incense to the East. Say:

> *By the Air that is Her breath, may you be reborn in joy.*

Raise the votive candle to the South, saying:

*By the Fire that is Her spirit, may your light shine
brightly in a new and even better life.*

Holding the votive candle, circle three times deosil for
rebirth, ending at North.

Replace the votive in the Spiral. Say:

Blesséd be _____.

Draw an invoking pentagram above the votive with the
wand or your finger. Say:

*You are a child of the Goddess, and if it be your
wish, may you be reborn into the Family of Wicca.*

Now sit by the altar for a while, remembering your
friend, her best qualities, your times together. If you feel
comfortable doing so, talk to your friend's spirit, telling
her how you feel.

Take the piece of paper and write or draw on it some
expressions of your feelings or wishes for her: her initials,
runes, hearts, pentagram, moons, happy face; whatever
feels right. Place it under the votive candle.

When your contemplation is finished, you can bless some
wine and raise a toast to her, or sing some fitting songs (*We
All Come from the Goddess, Hoof and Horn,* etc.). When
you have done this, face the altar. Say:

Great Mother Goddess, Great Horned God, and ye Mighty Ones of the four Quarters, thank you for attending this rite.

Ring the bell three times and say:

This rite is now ended, but may the loving energies continue to follow and bless _____ on her journey. So mote it be.

(If a Circle has been formally cast, it should now be formally opened.) Blow out the altar candles, but let the votive continue to burn all the way down, or burn it for several consecutive nights until it is completely gone.

Later, gather the rosemary, black stone, and paper talisman, and wrap them with the red string. Bury them together in the ground where they will not be disturbed. They can be put in the grave if there is one; it's an ancient widespread pagan custom to bury "gifts" with the dead to help them on their journey.

Bless a chalice of wine and hold it above the burial site. Say:

Blessed is the Great Mother, who gives life to the universe. From her we all proceed and unto Her we must all return. She is the Ground of Being that dwells within us, changeless, boundless and eternal, and Her love is poured out upon the Earth.

Pour the wine out upon the earth, and lay flowers on the top. Say:

Blesséd be.

We add to this ritual's "grave goods" symbols of the deceased's favorites — scraps of food (a feast of the deceased's favorites is nice afterwards), ribbons, a key, bits of cloth from well-worn clothes, a curl of hair if that's possible. Everything should be blessed before being buried with or for the deceased.

Several years ago, when a great-grandmother died, I wrote a song for her and then I wrote another one for everyone. If you like it, you can use it as it is; or feel free to change a few words to make it more specific and appropriate in your own circumstances. It lends itself very well to harmony.

Farewell, I Bid You

by Ashleen O'Gaea
Music transcribed by Lewis R. Saul

Chorus:
Farewell, I bid you on you way to Summerland.
May your crossing be easy on the tide.
I know the Goddess welcomes you with Her outreaching hand
The God will keep you safely by His side.

Verses:
You will not be forgotten on this Earth where you once stayed;
The lips that kissed you still will speak your name.
We who ran beside you, we still run where you once played.
And everything and nothing is the same.

Your spirit lives among us, and now that it is free
You guide us still: your life lights up the sky.
And we will follow you, follow the God across the sea,
For you only go the way we all go by (by and by).

The Gods extend to every Mother's child who comes a hand
Forever everyone with love They greet.
So fare thee well, I bid you, on your way to Summerland;
We were merry, and once more we'll merry meet (by and by).

8

LIVING MYTHICALLY

In his popular books and television series, Joseph Campbell advised "living mythically." We find this consistent with Wicca, and appropriate to family life. Of course it doesn't mean dressing in sandals and brandishing swords, or setting out on vacation without map or compass! So what does "living mythically" mean to a modern Wiccan family?

We interpret it to mean living life as an adventure. That sounds obvious — but how do you make an adventure out of making a bed or changing a diaper or anything else?

Nothing is wrong with imagining the aisle between the couch and the wall to be a strait fraught with monsters that can only be defeated with the vacuum cleaner, or the floor under the kitchen table to be the lair of a cyclops against which the only effective protection is a mop.

Nor is there anything the matter with offering yourself rewards: when you and Vinegar and Water have vanquished those Perilous Windows, you can feast with your comrades, Cookies and Tea!

It is profoundly true that the most important thing in any adventurer's life is home — the hearth and hearts for which adventure is undertaken in the first place. Whether you're safe at the table in your clan's Great Hall or sitting with companions around a fire at the mouth of a cave, there is still dinner to provide and share, literally and figuratively.

Heroes, heras and bards of old put a good deal of themselves into every meal they prepared — there was the hunt (or the gather or the scavenge) and the building of the fire, the defense of the fire and the turning of the spit, and the intimate relationship with Gods and spirits to be guarded as well. A mistake in dealing with any of these resulted in no evening meal at best, and a defeated quest at worst!

Most of us don't have to hunt or gather food from the wild now (although some supermarkets make a good approximation). Most of us can kindle and coax our cooking fires with a flick of the wrist. But we must still groom our relationships with Gods and spirits; we must not forget the God's willing death in the harvest of grain and game that serves life, or the Goddess' love that grows us all, season by season, life by life, year after year.

Like adventurers of old, we must guard our hearths wisely, but not harshly. It is not less true for us than it was for the wandering heroes and queens of old that the stranger who begs succor could be a Wise One. Neglecting to share what we have is still at least a rejection of opportunity.

The magical tools the strangers bestow in exchange for our hospitality are more subtle these days. No more (well, not as often, anyway) the talking harp, the righteous sword, the ever-full flask. But how full of healing is the heart that loves unconditionally? How fortunate is the long-forgotten favor finally returned, greater than it was granted or remembered? How much magic is in the courage of stopping to help the fallen when the path most easily taken avoids them?

Mystery is everywhere. Not just the mystery of what the driver ahead of us is going to do, either, but real mystery, with spine-tingling potential. Endless possibility does not well suit the bureaucracies in which we live: not the institutional bureaucracies, not our family bureaucracies. We've all learned a protective insensitivity. If we want to live mythically, we have to resensitize and re-orient ourselves in the widening world we are just rediscovering.

Almost all the cultural prejudice against Wiccan customs derives from the propaganda strategies used to conquer pagans as the various patriarchal empires were expanding. Even a few of the Ten Commandments (never mind The Rules today) seem ideally suited to suppression of Goddess-worshipping cultures.

Most of the prejudices against paganism encountered now are based on the uninformed observations and interpretations of foreign invaders; like the Romans, who measured every culture against their own and found most others lacking. (You may have noticed your neighbors taking the same attitude!) By patriarchal and increasingly monotheistic standards, it became impossible to accept European pagans as civilized; by those same standards, it's impossible for some people now to accept Wiccans as civilized.

Much as science fiction movies present alien worlds one-dimensionally — with extras all having the same clothes and the same hair and doing the same things, without schools or hospitals or grocery stores or parks and only the main characters showing signs of being well-rounded — our records of our religious ancestors' lives are conveniently biased toward the reporting conquerors' "superiority."

Sociologists today write about the age-old technique of dehumanizing the enemy to rationalize the torture, slaughter and enslavement of civilians. We are just beginning to loosen our grip on modern prejudices against the Germans and the Japanese, defeated almost 50 years since and much changed since then. We have not even begun to reform our prejudices against Witches, even though Witchcraft fell victim to the same propaganda techniques much longer ago.

As adventurers, this is what we face: an ignorant, frightened wilderness that just happens to be where we were born. Understanding it in this context, we don't have to take our families' (or society's or the fundies') anger and confusion personally. Many of us had to overcome a cultural aversion to the word *witch*, and for some of us this was difficult in spite of the Goddess' motivation. It's not going to be any easier for people who've spent their whole lives following — virtually worshipping— The Rules.

The rules by which many of us and most of our parents were raised are, according to Bradshaw (with whom we heartily agree), abusive rules. *Spare the rod, spoil the child,* that sort of thing. Fit in, hide your feelings; the pain is supposed to be tremendous. Once we understand that, though, we can erase those tapes so they don't play back whenever we're under stress.

Then, rather than responding defensively to questions, skepticism, disinterest, ridicule, accusation, and so on, we can discover the root fear and address it gently, as we'd approach a wounded animal. We don't guarantee this approach will be successful if your only goal is to change someone's mind, but a loving approach leaves our consciences clean, and it is healing to everyone concerned.

Sometimes the root fears are easy to calm. Several years ago, my mom heard some self-styled "witch" say on the *Tonight Show* that she celebrated the Summer's Solstice by dancing naked around a bonfire and burning money. Justifiably perplexed, Mom called and asked if that was what we did. Nope, I said, and we had a good giggle about wishing we had money to burn.

Sometimes the fears are harder to identify and assuage. Magic and meditation are both useful tools with which to control ourselves in difficult situations. If a family member is seriously aggressive or offensive, binding may help, but beware, for as you bind, so are you bound, and even the most carefully considered and worded binding spell is manipulative. We prefer spells along these lines:

> *Let the Goddess speak through me*
> *that what I mean they may clearly see.*
>
> *Show me the words that I can say*
> *so I may be understood today.*

Resolving conflicts in family relationships is one of the most difficult healings or quests any of us undertake. The obstacles are many. Family is a realm in which it is prudent to take Campbell's advice to live mythically — and to remember to follow your bliss, to answer your own callings, too.

We should not be any less prepared for our adventures across the landscape of family relationships than we are for any other adventure; it is not a less mythic quest. In fact, the myths from which our rites and spectacles are drawn are, broadly, about each generation's place-taking in the world family, about conflict resolution.

Realizing that, you can see that it just doesn't get any more mythical than family. Before every foray, we need to ground and center, collect and meditate with our tools, remember our purpose, bless ourselves.

When you take this trouble, not only are visits with family less stressful, you are also setting good examples for your children. We all hope to avoid making any major mistakes in bringing up our children. We all hope that when our kids are our age, their core relationships will be solid and affirmative, not draining or anxious. But we all know that they will encounter adventures in their lives, adventures on which we won't accompany them, though we hope to hear about them when next we gather together in the Great Hall (whether that's at Gramma's or in the Summerland).

The examples we show them, the constancy with which we keep our vows to enter Circles in perfect love and perfect trust, are among the tools they will use when they take up their own quests.

Years ago when *Close Encounters of the Third Kind* was a new movie (and we still liked to see new movies in theaters), Canyondancer and I were so taken with it that for the next few months, whenever we saw clouds like the ones in the movie, we drove up to the foothills and waited. The spaceships haven't come yet, and my left brain does not imagine they ever will.

Indeed, my left brain is deeply offended by suggestions that the work of ancient civilizations — Egyptian temples and pyramids, Stonehenge, North and South American mounds and cities — were engineered by aliens! I confess to being sternly intolerant of assertions that my ancestors were feeble of mind and body and spirit. As for the notion that giant figures fully visible only from the air must have been landing strips, I reject it, and take these for religious artifacts, geometric community offerings to the Gods.

My right brain is less political, and trusts not only that aliens might one day stop by for tea, but also that they would be wise and gentle people. Both my brains agree that any culture cooperative enough with time, energy, and resources for inter-planetary travel will have overcome voluntary aggression and be on peaceful missions of sociable exploration.

Those are the only bounds my right brain knows. Apart from trusting, knowing that the Nature of Life is peaceful — *behold, She is the Mother of all things, and Her love is poured forth across the universe, and love unto all beings is Her law* — there's no limit to my belief in possibilities.

Trust in this limitlessness is mythic. Before the Goddess, we are neither bound nor unbound, and as above, so below: the universe is neither bound nor unbound (something physics concludes, too). There are laws we must follow, of course, but they are not laws we can violate and be punished for breaking. They are laws that we cannot break, like the laws of three-dimensional existence. It's not a question of risking jail time for living six-dimensionally, after all!

Nor are the natural consequences of certain behaviors —broken bones or worse for walking off the edge of a cliff, for instance — punishments. Rain from rain clouds is not a punishment, it just is. We can explain it in terms of the laws of physics that science has articulated for us, and these laws apply equally everywhere. They do not depend on our "good" or "bad" behavior.

And yet we must choose to believe, choose to make it true, if we want to live mythically, that everything happens for a reason. We need to know the places of our lives well enough to recognize their similarities, well enough to see their patterns. We need to understand all the Worlds as part of the same cosmic psycho-biosphere.

We need to see signs and portents everywhere, and know that what we do matters in the World and to the World, because what we see and do *is* the World.

Physics offers an example. Watch your hand move through the air, and you can tell its speed and direction. But if you look at it from the corner of your eye, you can tell either which way or how fast it's moving — your perspective doesn't allow you to note both.

If you wave your hand around behind your head, where you can't see it at all, well, it could be going anywhere, at any speed. Studying micro-micro particles in photo-tanks, physicists find the same limitations — and they agree that until a particle's velocity or direction is measured, it could be going anywhere at any speed.

Here's another example that may help to make this clear, if it is not already so: J.R.R. Tolkien's *The Hobbit* and *The Lord of the Rings* trilogy has meant many things to many people. Some have taken these books to be an allegory about World War II. In an undergraduate thesis, I asserted that Bilbo's and Frodo's adventures and the natural laws by which they adventured offered proofs of Tolkien's own religious dogma, though the population of Middle Earth never referred to its gods or faith.

Tolkien himself insisted (like Freud?) that it was "just a story" for the kids. But the Christian Tolkien, like many Wiccans, was steeped in histories of all kinds — political, social, linguistic and mythic — and whether he was conscious of it or not, this opened his mind to the cosmic adventure. His books would never have been so popular if they had been just about World War II, or if they had been just a proof of religious thought. It was only because they weren't just allegory or proof that they could be allegory and proof too.

Until we choose to see a thing in a certain way, we have the potential to see it in an almost infinite number of ways. Perspective — visual or psycho-spiritual — is a matter of choice, and that is the practical as well as theoretical truth of most situations.

Is vacuuming a dull chore, or a way of banking the fire for the long, magical night? Is changing a diaper something to rush through holding your breath (okay, sometimes it is), or brave camaraderie? Without a flexible perception to allow her to recognize magic in mundane disguise, how far can any hera follow her quest?

In our experience, the best way to live mythically is to choose to live mythically, to put even the mundane tasks into a wider perspective. I make an effort to respect cows, for they are sacred to Cerridwen, yet I do not want to live like a cow, unable to cross the metal bars on the road and unable to distinguish between the real barriers and painted ones.

Society paints a lot of barriers on the road, many of them derived from patriarchal monotheistic systems (the other PMS). On the Wiccan quest to restore the Goddess' altars, literally and figuratively, that magical flexibility of perception is both our most important tool and the hardest to win.

For all of us, an important part of living mythically is testing the barriers. Are they real, or are they only paint? And if they are real, are they really impassable? Earth, air, fire, water, and spirit. No paint.

Respect the Goddess' boundaries, which are few and subtle; consider all the painted ones blasphemies or tests, and approach them accordingly.

The Explorer has learned this already, and learned it well, and yes, sometimes it causes trouble. We have told him (among other things) that he never has to accept brute force for legitimate authority — so he tangled with a teacher who believed that the most important lesson a student can learn is to do what s/he's told, without question.

Confronted with this — blasphemy? test? — we said that we would rather come to a hundred parent-teacher conferences than raise the Explorer to an other-directed manhood.

Of course there are compromises to make: sometimes a hero has to play along with giants or other monsters to escape them, or to earn the magical tools in their keeping. Sometimes a kid has to be still and do what the teacher says, whether it makes any sense or not. Learning how and when to compromise is a useful skill for any adventurer. Sometimes adults have to be still and do what the boss says, whether it makes any sense or not. The corollary is knowing when (and how) to stand unmoved by intimidation, to be undeceived by manipulation.

Legitimate (creative, win-win) compromise must take place within a framework of non-negotiable and clearly defined standards and values. Even if you can't meet your standards all the time, the efforts you make to meet them strengthen you, your children, and our community.

You don't set out on a quest without knowing either your objective or signs to recognize it. Your kid's childhood is that night around the fire when the Shaman (that's you) teaches the signs, describes the quest. If your own Shaman (your parents, Catholic school, whatever) was an imposter, then you'll have to find a real one, or be your own, and get the signs straight before you go on. A family and/or coven is a great hearth around which to gather for this.

The effort made to distinguish your standards from those by which you can be oppressed is equally, if not more, important. Your family will need to define its values in terms of your own Wiccan tradition. Because the God/dess speaks many languages, you might not put things as we do, but all Wiccans will address the same basic issues. Here's our conceptual framework:

An ye harm none, do as ye will. Love unto all beings is Her law. What you give to the world, the world will give back to you three-fold. This holds for attitudes, too: *as ye will, so mote it be.*

Ye shall be free from slavery. This requires emotional honesty and some political attention so you notice whether or not you are enslaved.

We'll be around again, so we like to keep it nice. The Earth, the political system. Kind of like cleaning up before you go on vacation so you can relax in a clean house when you get home again. (Nice to have a lasagna, literal or figurative, in the freezer when you get back, too.)

When Nature compels us, it's toward survival and creativity, toward babies and works of art and peace. If what you're doing gets in the way of survival or creation, it needs to be reevaluated. We have choices; that's evolutionary, too.

Creatures with our cerebral capacity for choice are unlikely to evolve in an environment that offers no choices, just as the opposable thumb wouldn't have evolved if there were nothing we could hold with our improved grasp. Brown moths don't turn white if there are no light-barked trees on which to hide.

The Universe is friendly. (On his deathbed, Einstein said that "Is the Universe friendly?" is the only important question. The Goddess answers that it is.) Life is complementary, not adversarial. This implies that teamwork is natural.

We don't give up any individuality when we contribute our individual talents and skills to the team — the coven, the community and so forth. Neither do we give anything up when we become one with the Goddess. In both cases, we don't fade away to make room for the Big Thing, we expand until we are the Big Thing.

We are naturally empowered. This is both a religious and a generational conviction. Idealism is a function of the conceptual cortex, which is one of our evolutionary specialties. It's biochemical, and we think that's wonderful because it implies that peace and love and trust are biochemical.

Paleo-anthropologists have given ample evidence that, while we're capable of it, violence isn't "our nature," it's a defense mechanism. We have created a world in which we live in constant need of defense! The systems by which we have organized our local and global life put us at emotional and material war everywhere. We are crowded like once gentle, now aggressive rats in a cage, reacting the same way to the same stimuli.

As much energy as you can relieve from anxiety can be used to enjoy life, and to work more powerful magic to help free your quest-companions; members of your immediate family or Iraqis or endangered trees or beasts.

Wicca is one of the few Western religions that calls brain chemistry sacred and gives you control over it in ritual. Talk about power to the people! You *are* God/dess; big responsibility, big satisfaction in accepting it. When you live in harmony with the Goddess, you find that you are living in harmony with each other and with yourself, too, for YOU ARE GOD/DESS.

You are God/dess. The rainforest is God/dess. Your husbands and wives are God/dess. The neighbors are God/dess. Your children are God/dess. The fundies are God/dess. (Technically, our pets are God/dess, too, and our youngest cat definitely channels Her Queen of Hel aspect.)

Families are God/dess, too, or can be, in Wicca. In this book, we've shared with you some of the ways that our family's life is Wiccan; some your family might already know, and some we hope you will come to know as fondly as we do. We hope, too, that your family will become more aware of its own traditions; the old ones and the ones yet to be.

In our growing understanding of God/dess, our family is growing, too, as you and yours will. And in the God/dess' love, we now bid you farewell; go in peace — merry part, and merry meet again! Blesséd be!

Appendix A

The Charge of the Goddess

Listen to the words of the Great Mother, Who of old was known as Artemis, Astarte, Isis, Cerridwen, Diana, Melusine, Brigid, and by many other names:

Whenever you have need of anything, once in the month — and better it be when the Moon is full — you shall assemble in some sacred place, there to adore the Spirit of Me, Who is queen of all the Witches; you who would learn magic but have not yet gained its deepest secrets, there will I teach you. And you shall be free from slavery, and in token that you are truly free, you shall be naked in your rites.

Sing! Feast! Dance! Make music and love, all in My presence, for Mine is the spirit of ecstasy, and Mine as well is joy on Earth, and love unto all beings is My law. Mine is the Secret of the Door that opens upon youth; Mine is the Cup of the wine of life, that is, the Cauldron of Cerridwen that is the holy Grail of immortality. On Earth, I give knowledge of the Spirit Eternal, and beyond death, I give peace, and freedom, and reunion with those who have gone before.

Nor do I ask aught of sacrifice, for behold: I am the Mother of All Things, and My love is poured forth across the Lands.

Now hear the words of the Star Goddess, the dust of Whose heels is the host of heaven, Whose body encircles the Universe:

I, Who am the beauty of the green Earth and the white Moon among the stars, the Mysteries of the waters and the Desire in all hearts, I call upon your souls to arise and come unto Me, for I am the Soul of Nature that gives life to the Universe. From Me all things proceed, and unto Me all things return.

Let My worship be in the heart that rejoices, for behold: all acts of love and pleasure are My rituals. Let there be beauty and strength, power and compassion, honor and humility, and mirth and reverence with you . . . and you who seek to Know Me, know that all your seeking and yearning shall be to no avail, unless you shall know the Mystery: that if that which you seek you do not find within, you shall surely never find it without. For behold: I have been with you since the Beginning, and I am that which is attained at the end of all desire.

This is the version of the Charge of the Goddess that we hear when we celebrate and work under the Full Moon — and the Charge that guides our understanding of the world and our interpretation of what happens in it. With the Threefold Law (that the energy you give to the world comes back to you "threefold") and the Wiccan Rede *(an ye harm none, do as ye will)*, the Charge directs us to live in the Goddess and according to Her will, in harmony with Nature and with respect for and deference to the life that has been here longer than we have. (Like most pagans, we try to learn from our elders, not annihilate them.)

Because Wicca is not dogma-dependent, we can't just tell our kids to memorize a set of rules. We have to help our children experience the world as we know it to be. Not many of today's Wiccan parents were brought up in the Craft, so we can't fall back on memories of growing up Wiccan when we wonder how to raise our kids. The Charge and other liturgical pieces are our sources, our collective memory.

We must value experience highly enough to give it to our kids, so that the Charge is an illumination and not the experience itself. But how do you translate these beautiful words into experience? By beginning with the basics, and forging a family lifestyle that reflects your own interpretation!

According to Webster, a charge is laid upon us with authority: we are obligated by it. The question is, what is our obligation and how can we fulfill it? Here are some of our understandings. Your family will build its own traditions of inquiry and interpretation as you ask yourselves what the Charge means to you.

With our needs, we are to assemble to adore Her. To do this, we must be aware of our needs, something not as simple as it sounds in this day and age. To be aware of your needs requires the joint effort of both sides of your brain, knowing and feeling.

It is best to assemble when the Moon is full, but many of us meet at the New Moon, and some of us meet at the Quarter Moons as well. Assembling once a month (at least) is a clear direction, with the exact time left to us.

When we meet, we adore Her Who is our queen, and She teaches us magic. We meet to learn magic whenever we have need of anything, from which we may fairly conclude that magic will help us supply our needs.

The Goddess promises and commands that we shall be free from slavery, and that in token of this freedom we are to be naked in our rites. Now, there are many forms of slavery, and many ways to be naked, just as there are many Wiccan traditions. Our nakedness, physical and/or emotional, is a token, a symbol of our freedom from slavery; our nakedness needs to be appropriate to the slaveries we overcome. If you grew up with a lousy body image, then physical nakedness may be appropriate (or an appropriate goal). If you grew up protecting family lies, then baring feelings and the family secrets might be a more meaningful nakedness. We can raise our kids to be comfortable with physical and emotional nakedness — honesty, love and trust — and they can be free from all slaveries.

We are commanded to sing and feast and dance, and make music and love, all in the Goddess' presence. You can — many of us do — interpret this to mean that we must do these things in every Circle. You can also take it to mean that whenever we do any of these things, we are invoking the Goddess.

Indeed, in the second half of the Charge, She asks us to behold — to witness — that "all acts of love and pleasure" are Her rituals. Hers is the Spirit of ecstasy, so when we are ecstatic, we manifest Her. Hers as well is joy on Earth, so that when we create and experience joy, we invoke and manifest the Goddess.

Love unto all beings is Her law, and to follow it, we must find Her love within ourselves and let it guide us all the time, not just when we are in formal Circle. She has told us to be naked in our rites, but the Charge does not limit the occassions on which we are to sing, feast, dance and show love unto all beings. These are, in fact, things we need to do, figuratively at least, in every aspect of our lives.

She does not ask us to sacrifice to Her, for Her love is poured forth across the Lands. We take this to mean that the natural cycles of life and death keep the energy flowing as it should, and that no additional sacrifices — no death that is not in the service of life — is either required or accepted. These cycles — birth, growth, death, and rebirth — operate in all the realms (planes, Lands, dimensions, Worlds) and their constancy, (expressed succinctly, *as above, so below*) is the One, the Whole, the substance and manifestation of Her love.

Her authority to call upon our souls to arise and come unto Her is that She is the life-giving Soul of Nature. From Her we come, and unto Her we shall return. In between, we are the Goddess in mind and molecule, for it was Her joy that created us all. You and I and all our kids are made of it, and to prove it, our bodies are 97% the Waters of Her womb.

In worship of Her, we are to rejoice; and all our acts of love and pleasure, from the brush of your cheek against the baby's to the time you give to your community, from sex to a great meal, are Her rituals.

Let there be beauty and strength, power and compassion, honor and humility, and mirth and reverence with you . . . This is one of the most meaningful elements of the Charge, and it tells us very clearly that these qualities are not opposites. Our social structure presumes that they are opposites, that the qualities paired in the Charge don't "go together."

The Charge not only reveals to us that these qualities are complements, but it obligates us to integrate them in our attitudes and behaviors.

So, what *we* find in the Charge is that the world is not as the patriarchs tell us. The truth about the world is not fully revealed in the Charge, for ours is a religion to experience, not to tell. The Charge describes the perspective we must take to experience the Goddess' truth. From this we can derive certain fundamentals about the world.

First, we must be aware of our needs. Starhawk has developed this idea, summing it up in the advice to follow the self to find the Self. But since we are all related in the Goddess, to be fully aware of our needs we must also be meaningfully aware of others' needs and cycles, including the planet's. We must make ourselves comfortable with magic, too, for magic is one tool with which we can meet our needs.

We must be naked — which means undisguised as well as disrobed — in our rites, and we must be free from slavery. Freedom from slavery requires recognition of enslavement; freedom from slavery is also a pre-condition of nakedness, because you can't be sure you're naked if you don't know what you look like, and you can't know what you look like if other people define your life.

Facing these issues — society's Guardians? — and exploring them honestly and thoroughly, resolving them with an awareness of the standards you hold, individually and as families and covens, and being satisfied with the source and substance of those standards, that's how we are all charged by the Goddess.

Love, in fact, is Her law: act lovingly toward all beings. Are mountains beings? Mineral deposits? Forests? Rivers? Oceans? Lava fields? Deserts? The atmosphere? Bugs? You don't have to agree in your intepretations with me or anybody else. You must make your own and take responsibility for them.

Keep beauty, strength, power, compassion, honor, humility, mirth and reverence with you, and remember that these qualities are not mutually exclusive. From this and the Goddess' rejection of sacrifice, be assured that life is not a vale of suffering, and pain is not your lot.

Something else to notice about the Charge is that it does not contain any "Thou Shalt Not"s. You do not need to be restrained by threat or prohibition — you come from the Goddess, Who is beauty and joy and mystery. Your life is not offensive to Her, and your pleasures on Earth are not illusory distractions from a separate spiritual reality.

She does not hide from you, but invites you to experience Her mystery and learn Her magic. She does not require aught of sacrifice, and She will not punish you when you die. Beyond death, She gives peace and freedom, and reunion with those who have gone before.

This is a very different understanding of human nature and the world than monotheistic traditions give. You're not shameful slime with slim hopes of attaining grace, nor is the world a vile, expendable stage upon which a cosmic battle between a supernatural "good" and "evil" rages.

Your life looks very different when you see it from the Goddess' perspective, which She shares in the Charge. That perspective has been withheld from you — from all of us — for several thousand years, and reconstructing it for yourself and your children makes an enormous task, one that is even more enormously worthwhile. And remember: if that which you seek you do not find within, you shall surely never find it in any book.

APPENDIX B

CORRESPONDENCES

Direction	East	South	West	North
Colors	white, blue, yellow	red, gold, orange	blue, green, aqua	brown, black, green
Tools	staff, wand	sword, athame	chalice, cauldron	pentacle, cauldron
Element	Air	Fire	Water	Earth
Time	sunrise, morning	noon	afternoon	night, midnight
Season	Spring	Summer	Autumn	Winter
Guardians	Zephyrs	Salamanders	Merpeople	Dwarves
Attributes	thought, imagination, inspiration	activity, passion, consummation	emotion, intuition	physical strength, death and rebirth

This is not an exhaustive table of correspondences. Most books about Wicca contain a table of correspondences, according to particular traditions and in varying degrees of detail. This table is meant to give you an idea of the sorts of correspondences Wicca makes among directions, colors, times of day, elements and so forth. Because this is a book for your family, this table is a simple one, suitable for Witches of any age. As your family and your practice of Wicca grows, you will add correspondences of greater complexity and personal significance to this brief list.

For detailed lists of correspondences — of plants and animals, for instance; or magical stones, runes, Moon phases and magic; you should consult other Llewellyn books which cover these subjects more particularly.

APPENDIX C

CATALOGUE SOURCES

We're not endorsing any of the catalogues listed here. We've seen all of them, though, and we think they're worth looking at, if only for the sheer pleasure of seeing "our" stuff in "their" catalogues. We have ordered from some of these suppliers, and our opinions are noted.

We're listing them as much to bring it to your attention that "we're everywhere" as for any other reason. Even if you don't buy anything from them, you'll get ideas for your family from all of them.

Shopping from catalogues is more than just finding the right thing in the right color. Every thing in a catalogue is an expression of a world-view. Every thing is a theme with potential variations. Every thing you see suggests a wide range of possibilities for change.

Look for symbols and interpretations of our tools, the Directions, the seasons, the Gods Themselves. Look for beauty and strength, mirth and reverence. Let your lateral thinking do the walking through the tantalizing pages. Let what you see fill your head and your life with ideas: Sing! Feast! Dance! Blesséd be!

Co-op America, 2100 M Street N.W., Suite 310,
Washington, D.C. 20063.

> Intriguing and practical folksy stuff.

Donnelly/Colt Catalogue, Box 188,
Hampton, CT 06247.

> Good buttons and stickers: **Robin Hood Was Right, No More Witchhunts.**

Dusty Miller, 14 Weston Road,
Strood, Kent ME2 3E2, England.

> Not all of us are Anglophiles, but if you are, you'll really like these. One of his catalogues is called *Effective Folk Magic Charms;* another is *Live-wood Partners and Occult Tools.* The catalogues are printed from hand-written masters and delightfully illustrated. Allow double-plenty of time because he's really busy, and ask for a list of his audio tapes, too. (Thanks to T.O. for bringing these to our attention.)

Museum of Fine Arts, Boston, Post Office Box 1044,
Boston, MA 02120.

> Reproductions, jewelry, etc.

Pickety Place, Nutting Hill Road,
Mason, NH 03048.

> Charms! Potions! A Pickety Place vetivert star hangs over our front door.

Pottery Barn, Mail Order Department, Post Office Box 7044,
San Francisco, CA 94120.

> Neat candles and good ideas.

Signals, 274 Filmore Avenue East,
St. Paul, MN 55107.

> The "catalogue for fans and friends of public television." Good quality.

The Smithsonian Catalogue, Smithsonian Inst., Dept. 0006, Washington, D.C. 20073.

> Ancientry for sale.

Storytellers, Post Office Box 7416, St. Paul, MN 55107.

> They sell hand-made Crone puppets. I bought a cup that says **Keeper of the Family Tales** and I don't let anybody else use it. They also sell an interesting-looking cooperative board game called "Lifestories."

Of Cabbages and Kids, S. Randall Converse, 630 Pickford St., Department CK, Madison, WI 53711.

> "Tapes, books and games [that] encourage such values as sharing, peaceful problem-solving and caring about each other and the world around us." We have a cooperative card game package that we enjoy.

Aristoplay, Ltd., Post Office Box 7645-C, Ann Arbor, MI 48107.

> Games based on ancient cultures, including one called "By Jove." They also sell a Fish-like card game about Greek myths and legends.

Ladyslipper, Inc., Post Office Box 3124-R, Durham, NC 27715.

> Music tapes, some of them specifically Wiccan.

Olivia Records, 4400 Market Street, Oakland, CA 94608.

> Music, jewelry and accessories, like Goddess figures.

GLOSSARY

adobe (uh-DOE-bee): A mixture of dirt, straw and water shaped into bricks and dried in the sun. Modern adobe bricks are made according to the ancient formula and stabilized (invisibly) with asphalt so they won't disintegrate in the weather. Bricks are about sixteen inches long, eight inches wide, and four inches thick.

Anglo-Saxon: Early English. Spoken from the 5th through the 11th centuries CE. Several cognates remain in modern English, many of them in popular use; it's not your French you should be excusing! The word *witch* comes from the Anglo-Saxon *wic,* meaning "to bend or shape," which is what Witches do with energy and reality. (Chaucer's language was Middle English.)

as above, so below: A Wiccan way of saying that natural laws apply universally and that our inter-connectedness makes all realms metaphors for one another.

astral: A name for the planes or dimensions of reality existing beyond ordinary sight and measurement. Some are personal and some universal.

athame (uh-THAH-may, AH-thah-may): A ritual knife, usually but not always double-edged, used to cast Circles and for other magical purposes; never used as a weapon.

Beltane: May Day. One of the two most significant Wiccan Sabbats. The traditional Maypole braided with ribbons represents the creative union (sacred marriage, heiros gamos) of the Gods and the many ways their fertility is manifest in our lives.

besom (BESS-um): The brushy part of a broom, the bristles. Sometimes used in reference to the broom as a whole.

between the Worlds: See *Worlds, Between the.*

beyond the veil: Beyond what we can see, hear, taste, touch or know intellectually. Ghosts and the vastness of the universe are both *beyond the veil.*

bolline: White-handled knife used for ritual cutting of cakes, cords, herbs, etc. Not a weapon.

Book of Shadows: The hand-written book of ritual, spells, charms, chants, journal entries, meditations, etc., kept by every Witch. Traditionally black-covered, the "B.O.S." is not shown to the uninitiated.

Brigid: Also known as "Bride" (breed) and "Imbolc." Non-Wiccans call it Candlemas. The Feast of First Fires, Brigid honors the Mother Goddess as well as the growing God at February first, as the Sun's return from Yule darkness can be noticed.

Bride (breed): See **Brigid.**

bound nor unbound, neither: At initiation, a Witch's inter-relationship with the Gods is symbolized with this phrase and dramatized when the initiate is loosely tied with a consecrated cord. Obligated by natural laws, it is impossible to break and therefore unnecessary to enforce.

censer: A covered incense burner that can be carried around the Circle.

Charge of the Goddess: One of the best-loved pieces of Wiccan liturgical material, the Charge was recomposed by Doreen Valiente for Gerald Gardner. Adapted by many traditions of the Craft, the Charge is instruction and direction, description, encouragement, promise, and mystery. (See also *Appendix A.*)

cauldron-luck: Pot-luck. When the Tucson Area Wiccan Network began to meet monthly in a public park so interested newcomers could meet us and break bread with us, we wanted people to know who we were and that we had a sense of humor, so we coined "cauldron-luck."

charm: Dramatic or material, a charm combines writing, speaking, and/or drawing with herbs and elemental symbols and calls upon/contains their power, directing it toward a goal like protection, health, or good fortune.

Circle: A ritually dedicated sacred space where Witches' rites are conducted "between the Worlds." Marked at least by psychic energy and the HPs' sword or athame, the border also supports "Quarter candles" at the compass points. It may also be marked with stones, more candles, drawn lines, or with an embroidered or painted mat. Once cast, a Circle may not be entered or left until a door, quickly resealed, is ritually cut. The psychic energy of a Circle is always grounded at the close of ritual and celebration, but the physical demarcations may be left in place if the Circle is on safe private property.

consensus decision-making: Listening to and caring about everybody's needs, expectations, ideas, concerns and objections before deciding any question. You still have to compromise, but your cooperation is acknowledged and everybody's needs, if not preferences, are met in the pursuit of a common goal. (See Starhawk's *Truth or Dare.*)

Cords of Life: A Mabon activity we've adapted from Starhawk's ritual. Use three- or four-foot lengths of cord and decorate them with dry seed pods, feathers, twigs, shells and symbolic bangles and charms from craft and party stores to represent your personal harvests. Variations — in your collection of decorations, the size, texture, length, and color of your cords, and in the way you put them together — correspond to the way the year's been for you. A really pleasant family or coven group activity that's an opportunity to talk about reaping what you sow.

coven (CUV-en): Traditionally, six couples and a leader; now, from three to fifteen Witches. Typically, a coven is an extended family and can help relieve the stress of wide separation from the multi-generational "clans" in which we evolved. Covens are autonomous and the High Priestesses are "first among equals." Covens are the basic unit of Craft organization.

covenstead: The home of a coven, the usual place of its meeting, usually but not always the home of the High Priestess.

cowan (COW-unn): Not Wiccan.

Crone: A menopausal or post-menopausal Wiccan woman. The time at which a woman assumes her Cronehood is intensely individual. Because our culture is unkind to age, we can be uncomfortable with its wisdom; the Crone is not fully appreciated today, but as 'boomers age, she will be.

Croning: A ritual to recognize, announce, and honor a Crone within a family and/or coven, and to introduce her and commend her to the Gods. A celebration of her accomplishments, her depth, her value, her potential (the energy of biological motherhood released to other nurturing and creativity), and her perspective.

Cross-quarters: The Solstices and Equinoxes mark the Quarters of the year; the other four Sabbats (Brigid, Beltane, Lughnassad and Samhain) are the Cross-quarters.

death in the service of life: Natural or willing death that contributes to the life of the group (tribe, species, planet, etc.). Predation and aging and seed-cycles in the wild; death in childbirth, rescue, defense of human culture, that sort of thing. Does not include war, murder, execution, sport, cruelty, or socio- or psychopathy.

Deathing: Sitting with a dying person and performing rituals to make his or her dying easier. May include chanting, singing, soothing, laughing, crying, opening chakras, anointing, burning candles and/or incense, reading and/or recitation. By ritual or improvisation, preparing someone for and guiding them through their death experience.

Dedication: A rite preliminary to initiation. Appropriate for young or beginning students not yet ready for First Degree, but prepared to make an initial commitment to further study and practice.

Degrees: Not academic levels, but recognition of experiential accomplishments and achievements. Some Wiccan traditions do not use a degree system; most but not all that do recognize three degrees. The description of each degree varies among Wicca's traditions, but very generally, a First Degree initiate may fully participate in all ritual; a Second

Degree initiate may also lead ritual; and a Third Degree initiate may also teach and conduct initiations and other rites, private and public. Degrees are not bestowed by any impersonal hierarchy, but by a Witch's own High Priestess and High Priest, who are personal witnesses to a Witch's confidence that s/he is ready for a deeper initiation. To all degrees it is up to the student to ask for initiation.

deosil: Clockwise, sunward. A ritual stage direction, and the most usual direction for a ritual procession or dance. The other way is called *widdershins.*

desire, end of all: In this context, "desire" is the basic set of mortal needs and senses by which you're aware of being separate from the Whole. The end of it occurs when in death or shamanic experience your consciousness expands beyond discrete individuality to Wholeness, which is Goddess.

elf-lights: Illuminated candle cairns welcoming the local "little people" to the area. First introduced by Tucson's Faerie Moon.

Eostara (yo-STAR-uh): Also called "Ostara" and "Eostre" (YO-stree). At the Spring Equinox, Eostara honors the balance of light and dark as the year continues to wax. Rabbits, early flowers and colored eggs are ancient symbols of the fertility and rebirth we celebrate at this time.

Esbats: Full or New Moon gatherings. Magic is generally done at Esbats rather than at Sabbats. Esbats are in honor of the Goddess, one of Whose symbols is the Moon.

evil: Bad vibes. Wiccans don't believe in any devil and tend to ascribe horrifically unacceptable behavior to ignorance, fear or brain damage. Like other energies, anger and fear can be raised and directed; they aren't regenerative energies that can survive without stimuli. The Wiccan understanding of "evil" is not supernatural, and is less conspiratorial and more holistic than Hollywood's and Christianity's models.

Five-fold Kiss: The source of our "blesséd be," a traditional blessing bestowed with kisses and the following words, which may vary among traditions:

Blesséd be thy feet, that walk in the way of the Gods;
Blesséd be thy knees, that shall kneel at sacred altars;
Blesséd be thy sex, without which we would not be;
Blesséd be thy breasts, formed in strength and beauty;
Blesséd be thy lips, that will speak the names of the Gods.

fundamentalist (fundy, fundie(s)): A politically right-wing religious conservative who believes that the whole and only truth about life, the universe, and everything is contained in the Christian Bible. Often aggressively evangelical, not interested in dialogue or other people's perspectives, and not much concerned with historical reality.

Gaian: Of Gaia, of the Earth; referring to the fact that the Earth is a living organism of which all living things are a part.

Gates, the: Metaphorical reference to the passage from life to death: upon death, a person passes *through the Gates;* in a near-death experience or life-changing crisis, one can *face the Guardian at the Gates.*

God, the: A personification of an aspect of life's energy, the Wiccan image of that which dies and is reborn. He is often depicted with antlers or horns to represent the game that falls to the hunter so the tribe may live. He is also seen as the Green Man, representing the grain and other plants that die in the annual harvest so that life can continue. Born from the Womb of Mother Earth at Yule,

He mates with the Goddess at Beltane, enjoys his prime through the abundant summer, willingly dies in fall's various harvests, and rules the Underworld from Samhain until Yule. The Sabbats are celebrated in honor of His life's cycles that encourage us and guide us.

Goddess, the: A personification of an aspect of life's energy; the Wiccan image of what is generative and eternal; the principle by and through which death becomes life again. Mother Earth, Mother Nature, Maiden, Mother, Crone. Her awareness is the source of our humanity; we are the vehicle of Her awareness. (See also *thealogy* and *Appendix A.*)

grave goods: A symbolic and magical collection of memorabilia, gifts and supplies for someone who has died; a pouch or packet of ritual credentials and tools for the spirit world. The goods themselves are buried or cremated with the deceased; it is their psychic energy that will equip the journeying soul.

Great Rite: The *heiros gamos*, or sacred marriage, of the Goddess and the God, recreated ritually in one of several ways, most commonly as a blessing of ritual wine by the HPs with her athame as her HP holds the chalice. On special occasions the Great Rite is performed physically — and privately — by a Priestess and Priest bonded to one another. Not to be confused with Hollywood images of pagan orgies, which are not a part of Wiccan life or worship.

ground and center: Collect yourself, focus on the ritual at hand, clear your mind of mundane distractions and concerns so your energy will be strong. Find the quiet center. Often achieved through meditation and/or visualization.

Guardians (of the Watchtowers): Elemental energies whose images combine the corresponding characteristics of the directions they symbolize. The Guardians of the Watch-towers are invoked as the Circle is cast to add elemental and directional strengths, protections, and inspirations to the proceedings. (See *Appendix B.*)

guided meditation: Read aloud or played on tape, a narration of an astral journey through self-awareness, or to a specific astral site to explore memory and other personal realms, or to meet with other souls/spirits to find or exchange information or work together. Used to discover alternative attitudes toward problems and issues, sometimes to change behavior, and to effect light trance states for relaxation and healing.

handfasting: A rite to recognize and bind a conjugal relationship for a year and a day, after which period the couple may part or renew their vows. A handfasted couple is not restricted by the limited roles culturally assigned in civil or monotheistic marriages. A handfasting can legalize a civil marriage when it is performed by Wiccan clergy who are heads of covens in jurisdictions where Wicca is recognized as a religion.

hera: Female protagonist on a mythic quest or adventure, literary or literal.

hero: Male protagonist on a mythic quest or adventure, literary or literal.

Holly King: Anglo-Celtic image of one of a pair of archetypical twins. Holly is the king of the waning year, who wins the duel at the Summer's Solstice; his brother Oak wins at the Winter's Solstice to preside over the waxing year. Their myth survives not only in Wiccan ritual but in folk literature, where Cock Robin's exploits conjure the older story; "Light and Dark twins" are basic characters in most mythic cycles. (See also *Oak King.*)

HP (aiche-PEE): Abbreviation for High Priest. We also use HPH for High Priest and Husband because sometimes High Priestesses and their HP's are married.

HPs (aiche-pee-ESS): Abbreviation for High Priestess.

HPMS (AICHE-pee-em-ess): Behavior in an HP or an HPs that is too high-falutin'.

initiation: Ordination in the Craft. Every initiated Witch can invoke the Gods and work magic in a Circle. Most traditions recognize self-initiations to First Degree; though many traditions recognize all degrees of other traditions, coven-specific initiations are still the norm. In traditions that use degree systems, initiations may be performed only by Third (or higher) Degree Priest/esses. The initiation is symbolic of a mythic quest, death and rebirth, and must be requested by a student or apprentice; it is not granted unless the HPs is satisfied with the student's work or commitment to study. Self-initiation is less formal, but requires an equal commitment and is undertaken no less lightly. (See also *degrees.*)

Kinging: A ritual recognizing, announcing and honoring a man's full maturity, and introducing and commending him to the Gods. For men who are beyond youth but not old enough to be Sages. Kinging is unique to Wicca (as far as we know), but it does not confer a clerical degree.

Lammas (Lahm-us): See **Lughnassad.**

Litha (LEE-ha, LEE-thah): Midsummer. The Summer's Solstice, the beginning of the Sun's waning toward Yule. Per Shakespeare, a night of magic and delight. A celebration of the prime of (the God's) life — the abundance of growth, the health of the herds and crops, the inviting weather — in full awareness of mortality.

little people: The indigenous spirits and legendary occupants of a given land and/or culture.

livewood: Wood or wooden articles inhabited by the benevolent spirit (Dryad) of the parent tree. Dryads can project clones of themselves into beads, staffs, wands, etc., if they are properly asked when the wood is collected. (See also *livestone.*)

livestone: Stones or stone articles inhabited by the benevolent spirit of the source stone (boulder, mountain, outcropping, etc.). (See also *livewood.*)

Lughnassad (LOO-nah-sahd): The Cross-quarter Sabbat balancing Brigid, Lughnassad is also called Lammas and the

Festival of First Fruits. Celebrating the first of the year's three harvest festivals (Mabon and Samhain are the other two) on August second, Lughnassad still bears the name of Lugh Longhand, a Celtic aspect of the God.

Mabon (MAAH-bohn, MAY-bohn): The Autumn Equinox, second of three harvest festivals. Mabon sees feasting to celebrate and give thanks for the success of the harvest. A good time to remember your local food bank.

magic: Non-ordinary activity or experience. You can work magic, you can witness magic, you can feel it around or nearby. It ranges in "size and shape" from love to ritual, from personal to local (or regional or global), from human to Gaian. It can be large or small, and while it certainly includes the candle, cord, rune and other magic we do in our Circles, it's not just that. In its broadest sense, magic is anything that amazes or delights you, answers a need beyond ordinary meeting or makes you cry "for happy." Yes, there is "bad" magic — magic that is coercive or manipulative, but creative, growth-ful magic is much stronger, and much more common. Wiccans do not do "bad" magic. (See also *Three-fold Law, evil.*)

Moons: See **Esbats.**

mundane: Something performed or perceived as unmagical, ordinary, every-day, material, practical, secular. The 9-5 ratrace and rent and PTA routine and its attendant concerns.

nitwitchery: Occasional or habitual inconsiderate behavior among Wiccans and other pagans which risks insult or injury to other Witches or pagans. Showing off. Loudly, publically or otherwise obnoxiously violating common etiquette. Self-aggrandizing exploitation of Craft knowledge or practice. (The term was, as far as we know, coined by an HPs in Tucson.)

non-ordinary: Out of the ordinary, following apparently different and often intuitive rules. Magical. Non-ordinary reality is not entirely subjective. (See also *astral.*)

Oak King: Anglo-Celtic image of one of the archetypical twins of Light and Dark. Oak is the king of the waxing year who is victorious in the duel at the Winter's Solstice; Holly is the king of the waning year who wins the battle at Midsummer. (See also *Holly King.*)

other-directed: Motivated mostly or entirely by other people's standards, needs and/or expectations, or according to assumptions about other people's standards, needs and/or expectations, without regard for or even knowledge of your own needs, feelings, values or thoughts.

occult: It means "hidden." You know those "hidden pictures" puzzles they make for kids? That's kind of how Wiccans see the world; but try calling them "occult pictures" and see how many you sell! It's a good word with a bad reputation.

pagan: It comes from the Latin *pagani,* which means "country dweller." It means non-Christian because country-dwellers were the last to be converted.

passages: Significant transitions. Biological (birthdays, hormones), geographical, emotional, social, political, etc., especially when archetypical and universal. Any transition or aspect of transition that is important to the person in transit. Families, covens, neighborhoods, governments, societies, and planets go through transitions, too, and it's appropriate to mark those passages as well.

patriarchal: Any social, economic, religious or other system or institution, concept or principle that's organized around or derived from the consideration of partners and children as property. We call it patriarchy because it developed after we figured out fatherhood; and individuals — female too! — can also be patriarchal.

perfect love and perfect trust: An idea, a goal, a metaphor, an expression of feeling safe as a part of Nature. (This implies not only that Nature is okay, but that being part of something is okay, too.) An attitude we choose to take, it doesn't mean gullibility, it means not assuming some right to get mad or even, even if it's in your face. It also means realizing that your worth does not depend on your individuality, and that giving yourself up to the Whole is safe.

PMS: Patriarchal Monotheistic System(s).

Quarter-calls: Invocations, sometimes rhyming, to the Quarters or directional powers. Calling the Quarters is one step in casting a Circle and part of preparing it appropriately before invoking the God/dess.

Queening: A ritual recognizing, announcing and honoring a woman's full maturity and introducing and commending her to the Gods. For women who are beyond youth but not yet Crones. Queening (introduced by Z. Budapest) is unique to Wicca, but does not confer a clerical degree.

raising energy: Increasing the energy level in a group for the purpose of directing and releasing that energy toward an agreed-upon goal or target. Methods include breathing in unison, chanting, dancing, and variations of those activities.

ramada: A Southwestern-style covered patio. Ours is four feet by eight feet with an adobe-brick floor and an arched redwood frame covered with lattice panels. In Spanish, the word means "arbor," natural or hand-made.

Rede, the Wiccan: *An ye harm none, do as ye will.* Witches pay more attention to harming none than to doing as we will, and the "none" we harm is all of life.

reincarnation: Recycling for souls. People have different ideas about how it works and who comes back as what, but Witches accept it because Nature obviously recycles all energy, including ours.

ritual: Choreographed and/or scripted/memorized worship. The set of gestures are worshipful in themselves, and they induce an altered state in worshippers. Ritual ranges from almost standard liturgical material to reverent personal habits, and usually includes some form of song (chanting, for example) and dance (circling the altar, for example). Most Wiccan ritual takes place inside a psychic temple that is erected ritually; i.e., in the same way each time and in the same way that other Wiccans use.

rockeries: Rock gardens or arrangements, natural or hand-built.

Rules, The: From *Making Sense of the Sixties*, PBS. Obey authority, conceal your feelings, fit in with the group, and don't even *think* about sex.

Rune, the Witches': A chant used to raise power, usually recited while walking or running a circle around an altar or within sacred space.

Darksome night and shining Moon
East, then South, then West, then North
Harken to the Witches' Rune
For here I come to call you forth!
Earth and Water, Air and Fire
Wand and pentacle and sword,
Work you all to my desire,
Hark you all unto my word!
Cords and censor, scourge and knife,
Powers of the Witch's blade,
Wake you all now unto life,
Come now, as the charm is made!
Queen of Heaven, Queen of Hel,
Hornéd Hunter of the Night,
Lend your power unto my spell,
Work my will by magic rite!
By all the power of Land and Sea,
By all the might of Moon and Sun,
As I do will, so mote it be!
Chant the spell and ***be it DONE!***

runes: Ancient alphabets used today for ritual and magic. Witches use several runes; the following are Old English:

A B D E EI F H I J K L
M N NG O P R S T TH U W Z

Sabbats: Solar holidays marking the Sun's course/the God's life through the year. The Solstices and Equinoxes are the four Lesser Sabbats; the Greater Sabbats, also called Cross-quarters, are Brigid, Beltane, Lughnassad and Samhain.

Sage: An elder Wiccan man, a male Crone.

Saging (SAGE-ing): A ritual recognizing, announcing and honoring a Sage within a family or coven, introducing him and commending him to the Gods. A celebration of his accomplishments, his depth, his value, his potential.

Samhain (SAW-wain): From the Gaelic *sam fuin,* meaning "end of summer." One of the Cross-quarter Sabbats; with Beltane one of the two most significant Sabbats on Wicca's liturgical calendar. Halloween. Wiccans are not afraid of death, we know it's just a return to the Womb of Life in preparation for rebirth. Samhain is something like a giant family reunion with the spirits of the dead invited and honored.

sealing a spell: Closing your work on a spell with a word or gesture to contain the energy you've put into it. Can be elaborate or simple.

S/self: With a capital *S,* the Wholeness of which we are all a part, a reference to the Goddess-aspect of your personality. With a small *s,* that part of you conscious of being an individual.

shamanic: Broadly, referring to experience of non-ordinary states of consciousness and exploration of the astral realms to which they are gateways. Involving non-ordinary perception, experience, or activity.

Sight: The "second sight," clairvoyance. May also refer to related "second senses" like "having a feeling" or "just knowing."

skyclad: Without robes; naked for ritual. (See *Appendix A*.)

sound energy: Energy raised by wordless sound — *ahhhh, ohhhh,* etc. — to release and direct toward a goal. Energy rises with the pitch and/or volume and may be released with a shout or with sudden silence.

spell: A rhyming direction of power, spoken over a symbol of the event or circumstance to be influenced. Also a symbolic act (such as writing a rune or design, lighting a candle, etc.) to direct energy to influence an event or situation.

'stead: See **covenstead.**

story blessings: Stories from or about ancestral and other non-ordinary realms. Vehicles to direct power from those realms into ordinary life. Often spontaneous.

Summerland: An astral place where our souls rest between incarnations. It encompasses the Underworld and several astral planes and a variety of states of mind and being. There we review what we learned in our most recent life and prepare for the next.

Suns: See **Sabbats.**

taboo: It's used to mean "forbidden" in our culture (and in this book), but a taboo can in its original context be an obligation as well as a prohibition.

tapes: A buzz-word for the conditioning we undergo as children. All the "you should"s and "you're just"s and "why can't you"s we heard between birth and school. Self-psychology involves erasing and re-recording "the tapes;" so does study for initiation.

thealogy: The study of Goddess and the relationships between Goddess and humanity; study of Wiccan and some other pagan philosophies and issues. Similar to theology, but having to do with a generative principle that is feminine rather than masculine, and proceeding from correspondingly different premises.

Three-fold Law, the: The understanding that the sort of energy we project into the world is the sort of energy we'll attract and use in our lives. This law is on a par with the laws of physics in that it is a native characteristic of life rather than imposed upon us by any supernatural being or composed for us in the interest of any institution.

together hug: A group hug. We say "together hug" when it's personal and intimate, like at home before bed, and "group hug" when it's more public, like at a picnic.

traditions: Sects of Wicca: Seax-Wicca, Gardnerian, Dianic, Alexandrian, Fairy, Family, Eclectic, etc.

trads: See **traditions.**

Vine God: A representation of the foliate God, a figure twisted from vines and dried in time for Lughnassad. Filled with foil-wrapped cornbread, it's consumed by fire in a ritual enactment of the the God's annual harvest-time death in the service of life. The cornbread is retrieved and shared as a symbol of our participation in the cycles we celebrate.

visualization: Seeing something in your mind's eye, whether your physical eyes are open or closed.

Watchtowers: See *Guardians of the Watchtowers.*

Wheel of the Year: A conceptualization of the solar year, marked by the eight Sabbats. Often drawn as a sort of ship's wheel.

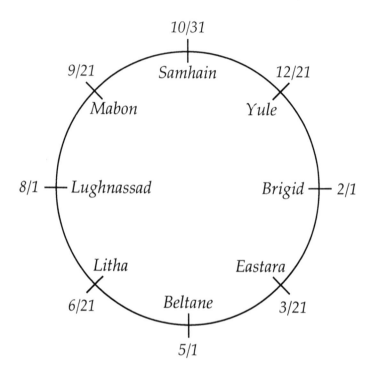

widdershins: Counter-clockwise. (See also **deosil**.)

Wicca: Traditional Anglo-European Witchcraft: pre-Christian, experiencing deity as a complimentary polarity, worshipping according to the cycles of the Moon and Sun. With roots in paleo-European cave culture, modern Wicca is a synthesis of many Indo-European and Romano-Celtic traditions. Now primarily an Anglo-Celtic religion comprised of several traditions or sects.

Wiccan Scripture: Nature. Everything from watching the squirrels bury nuts in the park to astrophysics — natural history and how it happens. The Natural model. There is no ultimate Book of Authority, but there are some really good shows on PBS, and every Witch has a personal Book of Shadows.

Weber bonfire: A biggish ritual fire in the barbecue in the absence of any other suitable fire pit, ring or place.

Wiccaning: A ritual invoking the Guardians and the God/dess to meet and bless babies born into the Wiccan community.

Wise Ones: Ancestral elders, heras, heroes, Guardians, aspects of the God/dess. Archetypical personifications of wisdom and experience.

Worlds, between the: Wiccans know the physical world is not the only world in which we live, that there are other realms and dimensions. The Underworld, the Spirit world, and other aspects of the astral, emotional, and psychological realms. When we worship in Circle, we are in a sacred space where the physical and the potential interface, where all times and dimensions interface, and where our rites and magic can draw upon their combined energies.

Witch: It comes from the Anglo-Saxon (Old English) *wicce* and *wicca,* which were pronounced *wee-cheh* and *wee-cha,* feminine and masculine respectively. The root, *wic,* means "bend or shape," Witches being those who do the bending and shaping, not those who are bent. Over the centuries, the pronunciation has changed and gender distinctions have disappeared; the modern word *witch* refers to both men and women.

wonder child: That part of our awareness that experiences the world as an amazing, wonderful, mythic place to explore.

That aspect of ourselves that works magic, the reservoir of perfect love and perfect trust. Characterized by gestalt, symbolic perception, "starlight vision" and lateral thinking.

younger self: Starhawk's designation of the wonder child. She calls its complement the "talking self." "Inner child" (Bradshaw) and "wonder child" (Jung) are other names for this part of ourselves.

Yule: The Winter's Solstice, when the Sun is reborn from the Womb of Earth. (See also *Oak* and *Holly Kings, Wheel of the Year, Sabbats* and *the God.*)

BIBLIOGRAPHY

Adler, Margot. *Drawing Down the Moon.* Boston: Beacon Press, 1979.

Boston Women's Health Book Collective, Inc. *Our Bodies, Ourselves.* New York: Simon & Schuster, 1973.

_____. *Ourselves and Our Children.* New York: Random House, 1978.

Bosworth, Joseph, and T. Northcote Toller. *An Anglo-Saxon Dictionary.* London: Oxford University Press, 1964.

Bradshaw, John. *Homecoming, Reclaiming and Championing Your Inner Child.* New York: Bantam Books, 1990.

Buckland, Raymond. *Buckland's Complete Book of Witchcraft.* St. Paul, Minnesota: Llewellyn Publications, 1986.

Budapest, Zsuzsanna. *The Holy Book of Women's Mysteries complete in one volume.* Berkeley, California: Wingbow Press, 1980, 1989.

Campbell, Joseph. *Historical Atlas of World Mythology.* New York: Perrenial Library, Harper and Row, 1988.

Capra, Fritjof. *The Tao of Physics.* New York: Bantam Books, 1984.

Castaneda, Carlos. *Teachings of Don Juan: a Yaqui Way of Knowledge.* Berkeley: University of California Press, 1968.

Crowley, Vivienne. *Wicca: The Old Religion in the New Age.* Wellingborough, Northamptonshire, England: The Aquarian Press, 1989.

Cunningham, Scott. *Wicca: A Guide for the Solitary Practitioner.* St. Paul, Minnesota: Llewellyn Publications, 1989.

_____, and David Harrington. *The Magical Household.* St. Paul, Minnesota: Llewellyn Publications, 1989.

_____. *The Magic in Food.* St. Paul, Minnesota: Llewellyn Publications, 1991.

_____. *The Truth About Witchcraft Today.* St. Paul, Minnesota: Llewellyn Publications, 1988.

Dreikurs, Rudolf, M.D., with Vicki Soltz, R.N. *Children: the Challenge.* New York: E.P. Dutton, 1964, 1987.

Farrar, Janet and Stewart. *A Witches Bible Compleat, combined volumes I and II.* New York: Magickal Child Publishing, 1981, 1984.

Forward, Susan, and Craig Buck. *Toxic Parents.* New York: Bantam Books, 1989.

Hawking, Stephen W. *A Brief History of Time.* New York: Bantam Books, 1988.

Kubler-Ross, Elisabeth. *On Death and Dying.* New York: McMillan, 1970.

Moody, Raymond A., Jr., M.D. *Life After Life.* New York: Bantam Books, 1977.

Potts, Billie. *Witches Heal.* Ann Arbor, Michigan: DuReve Publications, 1988.

Smith, Lendon H., M.D. *The Children's Doctor.* Englewood Cliffs, New Jersey: Prentice Hall, Inc., 1969.

_____. *Improving Your Child's Behavior Chemistry.* New York: Pocket Books, 1976.

Sousa, Mrs. Marion. *Childbirth at Home.* New York: Bantam Books, 1977.

Starhawk. *The Spiral Dance, a Rebirth of the Ancient Religion of the Great Goddess.* San Francisco: Harper & Row Publishers, 1979.

Stone, Merlin. *When God Was a Woman.* San Diego, New York, London: Harcourt, Brace, Jovanovich, 1976.

Tolkien, J.R.R. *The Hobbit.* New York: Ballantine Books, 1986.

_____. *The Lord of the Rings.* New York: Ballantine Books, 1971.

STAY IN TOUCH

On the following pages you will find listed, with their current prices, some of the books now available on related subjects. Your book dealer stocks most of these and will stock new titles in the Llewellyn series as they become available. We urge your patronage.

To obtain our full catalog, to keep informed about new titles as they are released and to benefit from informative articles and helpful news, you are invited to write for our bi-monthly news magazine/catalog, *Llewellyn's New Worlds of Mind and Spirit.* A sample copy is free, and it will continue coming to you at no cost as long as you are an active mail customer. Or you may subscribe for just $7.00 in U.S.A. and Canada ($20.00 overseas, first class mail). Many bookstores also have *New Worlds* available to their customers. Ask for it.

Stay in touch! In *New Worlds'* pages you will find news and features about new books, tapes and services, announcements of meetings and seminars, articles helpful to our readers, news of authors, products and services, special money-making opportunities, and much more.

Llewellyn's New Worlds of Mind and Spirit
P.O. Box 64383-591, St. Paul, MN 55164-0383, U.S.A.
* * *

TO ORDER BOOKS AND TAPES

If your book dealer does not have the books described on the following pages readily available, you may order them direct from the publisher by sending full price in U.S. funds, plus $3.00 for postage and handling for orders *under* $10.00; $4.00 for orders *over* $10.00. There are no postage and handling charges for orders over $50.00. Postage and handling rates are subject to change. UPS Delivery: We ship UPS whenever possible. Delivery guaranteed. Provide your street address as UPS does not deliver to P.O. Boxes. UPS to Canada requires a $50.00 minimum order. Allow 4-6 weeks for delivery. Orders outside the U.S.A. and Canada: Airmail—add retail price of book; add $5.00 for each non-book item (tapes, etc.); add $1.00 per item for surface mail.

FOR GROUP STUDY AND PURCHASE

Because there is a great deal of interest in group discussion and study of the subject matter of this book, we feel that we should encourage the adoption and use of this particular book by such groups by offering a special quantity price to group leaders or agents.

Our Special Quantity Price for a minimum order of five copies of *Family Wicca* is $29.85 cash-with-order. This price includes postage and handling within the United States. Minnesota residents add 6.5% sales tax. For additional quantities, please order in multiples of five. For Canadian and foreign orders, add postage and handling charges as above. Credit card (VISA, Master-Card, American Express) orders accepted. Charge card orders only ($15.00 minimum order) may be phoned free within the U.S.A. or Canada by dialing 1-800-THE-MOON. For customer service, call 1-612-291-1970. Mail orders to:

LLEWELLYN PUBLICATIONS
P.O. Box 64383-591, St. Paul, MN 55164-0383, U.S.A.

Prices subject to change.

THE TRUTH ABOUT WITCHCRAFT TODAY
by Scott Cunningham
Here is the first real look at the facts about Witchcraft and the religion of Wicca. For centuries, organized religions have perpetrated lies about the ancient practice of Witchcraft, and to this day many misinformed people think Wicca involves worship of the Devil, sex orgies, and drug use. It just isn't so! As Cunningham plainly states, the practice of magic is not supernatural or Satanic. Witches and folk magicians are only utilizing, through timeless rituals, natural energies found within the Earth and our bodies to enrich life by creating positive change.

If you are completely unfamiliar with Witchcraft, and have wondered exactly how magic works, this book was written for you! In a straightforward, easy-to-understand manner, Cunningham explains the differences between folk magic, ritual magic, ceremonial magic, and religious magic. He describes the folk magician's "tools of power" crystals, herbs, candles, and chants—as well as the ritual tools of the Wiccan: the athame, cauldron, crystal sphere and pentacle, among others. He also provides an excellent introduction to the practice of magic by delineating two simple folk magic spells, a circle-casting ceremony, and complete Wiccan ritual.

0-87542-127-X, 208 pgs., mass market $3.95

WHEEL OF THE YEAR
Living the Magical Life
by Pauline Campanelli, illus. by Dan Campanelli
If you feel elated by the celebrations of the Sabbats and hunger for that feeling during the long weeks between Sabbats, *Wheel of the Year* can help you put the joy and fulfillment of magic into your everyday life. This book shows you how to celebrate the lesser changes in Nature. The wealth of seasonal rituals and charms are all easily performed with materials readily available and are simple and concise enough that the practitioner can easily adapt them to work within the framework of his or her own Pagan tradition.

Learn to perform fire magic in November, the secret Pagan symbolism of Christmas tree ornaments, the best time to visit a fairy forest or sacred spring and what to do when you get there. Learn the charms and rituals and the making of magical tools that coincide with the nesting season of migratory birds. Whether you are a newcomer to the Craft or have found your way back many years ago, *Wheel of the Year* will be an invaluable reference book in your practical magic library. It is filled with magic and ritual for everyday life and will enhance any system of Pagan Ritual.

0-87542-091-5, 176 pgs., 7 x 10, illus., softcover $9.95

BUCKLAND'S COMPLETE BOOK OF WITCHCRAFT
by Raymond Buckland

Here is the most complete resource to the study and practice of modern, non-denominational Wicca. This is a lavishly illustrated, self-study course for the solitary or group. Included are rituals; exercises for developing psychic talents; information on all major "sects" of the Craft; sections on tools, beliefs, dreams, meditations, divination, herbal lore, healing, ritual clothing and much, much more. This book unites theory and practice into a comprehensive course designed to help you develop into a practicing Witch, one of the "Wise Ones." It is written by Ray Buckland, a very famous and respected authority on Witchcraft who first came public with the Old Religion in the United States. Large format with workbook-type exercises, profusely illustrated and full of music and chants. Takes you from A to Z in the study of Witchcraft.

Never before has so much information on the Craft of the Wise been collected in one place. Traditionally, there are three degrees of advancement in most Wiccan traditions. When you have completed studying this book, you will be the equivalent of a Third-Degree Witch. Even those who have practiced Wicca for years find useful information in this book, and many covens are using this for their textbook. If you want to become a Witch, or if you merely want to find out what Witchcraft is really about, you will find no better book than this.
0-87542-050-8, 272 pgs., 8 1/2 x 11, illus., softcover $14.95

THE MAGICAL HOUSEHOLD
Empower Your Home with Love, Protection, Health and Happiness
by Scott Cunningham and David Harrington

Whether your home is a small apartment or a palatial mansion, you want it to be something special. Now it can be with *The Magical Household*. Learn how to make your home more than just a place to live. Turn it into a place of security, life, fun and magic. Here you will not find the complex magic of the ceremonial magician. Rather, you will learn simple, quick and effective magical spells that use nothing more than common items in your house: furniture, windows, doors, carpet, pets, etc. You will learn to take advantage of the intrinsic power and energy that is already in your home, waiting to be tapped. You will learn to make magic a part of your life. The result is a home that is safeguarded from harm and a place which will bring you happiness, health and more.
0-87542-124-5, 208 pgs., 5-1/4 x 8, illus., softcover $8.95